Knitting and Knowing: The Threads of a Singular Life

ISBN 978-1-935751-07-6

Published by
Scribbulations LLC
www.scribbulations.com

Printed in the U.S.A.

To Joan —

I hope you enjoy my "story" and like all my ~~entimate~~ details as much as I enjoyed putting it together.

Love,

Arlene

Knitting and Knowing

The Threads of a Singular Life

Preface

My father took a picture of me when I was a young girl in 1938. I am wearing a lovely hand-knit cape and hat. Behind me are old black cars with running boards. The street is in Clifton, New Jersey, and I am standing in front of the Sacred Heart Catholic Church where I have just been to Mass with my parents and older brother. I cherish this photograph because I am smiling and look happy, maybe even a little shy.

My mother knit the ensemble. Years later when I asked her about it, she said it had been ripped out because in those days they reused the wool for other projects.

I learned to knit from my mother. When I was in high school, I made argyle socks with many bobbins, and I continue to knit to this day. It is always a happy pastime for me.

Knitting can be complicated with some knotty skeins. In my story I have knit together many multicolored, often difficult, often joyful, knotty threads of my life. Some threads come from my essays, but many come from my journal writings.

Be forewarned: honesty is a strong suit of mine.

Writing and reading memories evoke deep feelings. I hope my remembrances touch you in the reading as they touched me in the remembering.

Beginnings (1935 - 1956)

Mania and Back to Sanity

My adult life started when I was twenty-one and had to have shock treatments in a mental hospital. In those days doctors called my illness "manic-depressive." Now it is known as bipolar disorder.

I was newly hired as an English teacher in my hometown through the efforts of my father, who was friendly with a man on the Board of Education. The school was overstaffed and so I was not given a homeroom. It was hard not having a home, carrying a heavy briefcase with books and other paraphernalia for teaching English to ninth graders. The teachers' room became my home base.

Then the event that would influence my life for many years happened. I was young, attractive, somewhat shy, and loved by parents and friends when I began to feel more and more out of sorts. I was feeling happier and happier, more and more manic (a word not used in everyday conversation in the late '50s). At a wedding, I put my shoes on the bridal table to dance and was scolded. The bride and her party were angry at me. Did I care? Not very much, being so HAPPY.

My parents took me to a local doctor; I had never been sick. He gave me some pills for my mental state, and I began taking them. My mother did not approve of pills for much of anything: she being a strong, healthy Italian woman. She told me to stop taking the pills and "fight" the illness myself. And so I did.

I began to be afraid of work. I cried as I drove my car to the junior high school where I was teaching. Once I was observed by the principal, who was suspecting that something was not right with me. I still remember that day doing a "lay-lie-laid" exercise that even now, as an adult, confuses me. A student asked what "day of infamy" meant, and I flubbed around because I did not know. It was embarrassing to me, a young twenty-one year old.

When it became impossible for me to continue, my father told me to quit. I lay around the house that winter and, in the spring, got a job in a men's clothing store in Passaic, New Jersey. Then I learned that I could get my teaching job back in the fall; this time, teaching sixth grade in an elementary school.

Before the holiday season, starting after Thanksgiving, that strange but familiar feeling began again, this time more manic—singing/screaming Christmas carols for the whole school to hear. I did not return after the Christmas vacation, and in February, my parents with my fiancé, Jim, drove me to a private sanitarium. I had just gotten engaged, a February wedding was planned, and I had put a deposit down on a wedding dress.

As the three of us stood in the lobby, I was told I had to remove my engagement ring. I couldn't take it into the building with me. I became terrified. I was frightened walking alone with *strangers* into that massive, stone building. The orderlies escorting me said that if I tried to run away, I would never be allowed back.

My first roommate disappeared, and I never saw her again. Did she run away? I never knew. When I asked, the orderlies would shrug.

They said I would not be given shock treatment, but they lied. I can still recall the calm feeling I had lying on a cot in the hall before the treatments, much like the scene in *One Flew Over the Cuckoo's Nest.*

Awakening after each treatment tied down to the bed, being given orange juice with a straw, and then eating fabulous breakfasts with many others, I gained twenty pounds! I developed a crush on a Jewish boy who liked asking me questions about saints. We would sit together outside on the stone steps and talk.

Once a man asked if I had lots of hair there (pointing rudely). And once when I was sitting on the toilet, a man yanked the door open and yelled, "I found her. She's on the toilet." The group was going somewhere and they could not find me. I was so embarrassed, mortified in my innocence, thinking sitting on a toilet was private.

During my two-to-three month stay, my fiancé visited me frequently. Braving a bad snowstorm, he came on the day planned for our wedding.

My parents were so ashamed of my breakdown that they visited with my future in-laws and said the engagement could be broken off, that Jim did not have to marry me. Jim said, in front of both sets of parents, breaking our engagement was out of the question, that he loved me greatly and would marry me when it was time.

I was a young, innocent, virginal, Catholic girl smacked alongside my head. I had been a cheerleader and a good student, and was president of my college sorority, so how could this shame happen to me?

When I was released, I went back to my teaching job and finished out the school year. Once a boy said, "We know what happened to you." I just smiled at him and looked away.

Did the whole world know I was crazy? How could I live the rest of my life with such embarrassment?

I would cry heavily while I showered before a dinner or movie date with Jim. Those days were hard. The passing of time helped, like mourning the death of a loved one. I was mourning the death of my innocent ideas and enthusiasms about my "perfect" life.

The next year Jim and I married in July, and I began my third year teaching at the same school. I got pregnant very quickly. (Our first child was born before our first wedding anniversary.) In those days if you were pregnant, you could not teach after the fourth month, and so I said goodbye to my class at Christmas time.

The parents gave me lovely gifts. A handmade knitted Humpty Dumpty hung on our first Christmas tree, and it hangs on my Christmas tree to this very day more than fifty years later. Parts of a beautiful pink and blue wool baby blanket trim my summer bedspread even now.

And so I left behind my terrible experience and went on to raise five children with the love and help of my husband.

But I am getting way ahead of my story: of my youth, my loves, my marriage, the illnesses, and the sometimes special and often ordinariness of my life.

A Scared Little Girl

I am in my bed; I'm about seven, and my mother and father are not home. I was sleeping and now I'm awake. As I lay here on my stomach, I begin to feel afraid. I wonder who's downstairs. I wait, listening for a noise. If I do hear anything, I will be terrified because I am alone in the house; I don't know where my big brother is. My bedroom door is open, and I cannot bring myself to look down the hall because something might be there, a leering, horrible thing, ugly and angry.

I don't move; I am paralyzed. I begin to feel my body getting smaller; it is getting tiny. My head is the same, my brain is the same, but my body feels smaller and smaller, almost not there.

I hear voices downstairs: Mommy and Daddy. Good, I am safe, I think. And yet I know, on some not-understandable level, that I'm still not really safe. Sometimes Mommy yells and scares me.

I listen to know whether they will come upstairs. I want to tell them how scared I get when they are not here, and I am alone in the house in my bed, but I won't. I am afraid of my older brother mocking me and know that my parents do not like it when I say I am afraid of something. They always tell me there is nothing to be afraid of. I don't believe them. They don't hear what I say. And because they are older and smarter, I begin to think they know better. So why am I afraid so often?

This is crazy-making stuff. I stop telling them my thoughts. I begin to think there is something wrong with me. They don't cuddle with me and say, "There, there, I'm here," when I tell them I am afraid, so I begin not to tell them my feelings.

Once when I sat on a hot waffle iron that was on a chair, they said I was brave as they rubbed Vaseline on my backside. My mother would tell me what a brave girl I was years after the incident, which I never remembered. Was it because I did not cry? I began to think I was brave.

In my late twenties, after the bout with mental illness, my first psychiatrist asked me why I had chosen to experience so much pain in delivering a baby through natural childbirth, and I told him that I liked thinking that I was brave.

Now looking back on the awareness of myself shrinking while I lay in bed, I understand that my mind was learning how to be crazy. I thought my body was really getting small (that is exactly how it felt), and I might disappear entirely and never be found again, or worse, found in my teeny-tiny shape, much like the shrinking man. Would they build a dollhouse for me to live in?

I am glad I still have that memory because thinking of it has helped me to understand some of my old emotional problems. My mother would often say, "You were dreaming" about an event that happened in my life. Once I kept talking about a greenhouse we used to visit, and although my mother would say, "You were dreaming," a few years later my father told me, "You were right, we did visit an acquaintance who lived next to a greenhouse."

I knew then that most of the things I thought had happened did really happen, since I always remembered my dreams and knew they were dreams, not my real waking life.

Ice Skating

I loved ice skating when I was a young girl. There was a park with a small pond in front of my high school. When my father was a boy, there were horse races there and the pond was called Racys. From certain high school windows you could see the park and the pond. My best friend and I would cut classes on a clear, winter day and go ice skating. We felt very brave. No one ever noticed; we never got in trouble. We laughed about being truant because we were both college prep students.

I had figured out a foolproof way of cutting classes. I would stay in the bathroom while my homeroom teacher, Miss Johnson, was taking attendance so that my name would be put on the absentee list that circulated the school. I then went to whatever classes I wanted, and if I skipped a class, I was "absent," wasn't I?

Sometimes Miss Johnson would see me in the halls and angrily yell, "Arlene, I marked you absent!" I would tell her I was sorry but I was late coming to school. I was a good enough student that no one bothered me. I skipped classes my whole senior year and had the best times. I would even babysit and make some easy money sometimes, telling the mother I was able to get out early.

My best friend, Corinne, and I would go horseback riding. The stables were in the next town and either we bused there and back or a friend would drive. I never understood why my parents would not buy me a horse. After all, we had a garage where the horse could stay and I would take good care of it, I pleaded.

You would think I was a real daredevil and naughty; the truth is I was shy and frightened much of the time. But I was smart. My father would have been an engineer except he got my mother pregnant with my brother, so he quit NJIT (in those years, Newark College of Engineering) in his third year to marry my mother and get a job. My grandmother was so humiliated that she would not go to their wedding; she even dyed my mother's white wedding dress black after the wedding. This was in the '30s and my mother's family was Italian and ashamed, yet proud. What a different world we live in today.

Racys pond is still there today and is still used for skating—a lovely park in a lovely city.

Lessons in High School

When I was in high school, I wrote a short story for my creative writing class that had to do with a family fight. It was about a father slapping a daughter because of a snide remark she made and the daughter running away to a friend's house. She sees her error by noticing how dysfunctional (another word we did not use in the '50s) her friend's family is, and on that basis, decides that her family is okay, even her father.

She goes home and all is well. The mother is happy her daughter is home, and her father apologizes, hugs her tightly, but makes her uncomfortable with his overly emotional tears.

This story was written when I was sixteen and had a romanticized idea of family life. I wanted to be away from my over-protective parents. I wanted to be away from my life, out of the passions and confusions of sexuality and virginity and boys and girls and teen years. The slap had really happened to me except I changed the story line to make it fiction. I used what had been real and wrote about it in a way to protect my parents who would be hurt if they knew my negative feelings. The teacher gave it a *B* and said I needed a better title for it.

My last writing assignment was called "My Philosophy of Life." My teacher told me the essay I wrote was good enough to submit to Scholastic Magazine in my senior year. I had different teachers in my senior year, and no one encouraged me about my writing. I never sent the essay in and regret it to this day. Its title was "Live and Learn."

That creative writing class in my junior year started me on my love of writing: putting on paper the thoughts and ideas in my mind. Writing and knitting are my two passions to this day! I am still writing, and I entertain knitting friends at my house twice a month.

Senior Prom Angst

I have two memories of my Senior Prom. One was that as I descended the stairs in my strapless ball gown, with all the nervousness and movie-star acting I could muster, I dropped my purse! Talk about a stage entrance: my date looking at me. Just when I wanted it all to be so perfect, I bungled it. It was embarrassing, but now I am able to think it's funny.

The second memory is of my father having to cut the tag off my date's jacket. It was rented and my date Bob had not noticed it. Was he nervous, too? He was a junior and younger than me; we were going steady.

We stayed at the gym where the prom was held for a dance or two, and then a group of us drove into New York City and went to the Copacabana night club, where someone snapped pictures of us. I look happy and smiley.

My parents were old-fashioned and did not want me going steady. I secretly wore Bob's little gold football charm under my blouses. Once when my father was standing over me as I sat at my desk doing homework, he spotted it. "What's that?" he asked.

"Bobby's football," was my hesitant reply.

"Are you going steady with him?"

I told him "Yes."

Here I am at The Copacabana,
(with my friend Ralph—not Bob)
on the town after the prom.

He said something about he and my mom not approving, but I knew they liked him. Bob had come down the shore with us for a few days' vacation once and had slept with my brother. I was Catholic in those days, so we were pretty innocent and never really had sex, although we touched one another.

I knew I would never marry him. I wanted an educated man, someone who went to college. I would tell him that when we talked about getting married. I think he really loved me, and we were kids learning together. I continued dating Bob my freshman year in college because I was commuting.

Almost ten years later when I was married and expecting a second child, he called me and I invited him to visit me. I was nervous in those days about scandal (who might be watching a man entering my house while my husband was at work?), so we sat on lawn chairs in the driveway under my baby's window, in case she woke, and we talked. He wanted me to know that he was getting married to a nurse. I was happy for Bob and was pleased that he had wanted to let me know.

We truly cared about each other.

I still hear stories about him since I am living in the same town. A mutual friend says he speaks well of me. I usually say, "He was a lovely boy."

We double dated with my best friend. Gentle and fun times, but who knew then how fast those days would move and how quickly fifty years would pass? Happy days, happy memories.

My Dad Needed New Tires

When I became a young adult, we gave my dad gifts for his birthday. They were the usual things: ties, a bathing suit, sweaters, and the like.

One year, some days after his birthday, he was stressed about something. We were all talking about his birthday gifts, when he shouted, "I need new tires for my car. That's what I needed for my birthday, new tires!"

To this day many years later, I remember his anger, his angst telling us the way he did. I remember feeling sorry for him. This was not typical of him; he never displayed anger or fear. Maybe he was feeling financially burdened. Why didn't any of us know? Why didn't he ever ask for what he needed or wanted?

Of course if he had, I would not be remembering this story because we all would have given him money for new tires. Wouldn't we?

Men Fishing

One day my father, brother, and I went fishing at the lake where we used to vacation for a few weeks. The house was on the lake, high above it, and there were steps leading down to the dock. Most of my memory of the lake comes from pictures of me as a little girl having her hair brushed on the dock or standing in a rowboat.

This particular day, the three of us went into the rowboat to fish. Both my brother and father had fishing poles. Since there weren't three poles, my father gave me a stick—a tree branch, with its limbs shaved off and a strong string attached. The end of the string had a hook on which I learned to spear a worm and remove any fish caught.

The fish would eat the worm so delicately that it was able to eat and run before I even knew it was nibbling. I remember I was the only one who caught a fish—the only one—with my little, baited stick! I was able to remove the fish, and we put it in a pail of lake water that I kept watch on all afternoon. I watched that fish swim in circles; I talked to it. I have no memory of what happened to my fish. Maybe my dad helped me ease it back into the lake, or maybe he did it himself.

I don't recall ever eating any of the fish we caught. But I have carried the memory of my success that day all my life. It still brings me a kind of female pleasure: my dad and brother were both so smart, but I caught the fish!

Friendly Porches

Where I grew up, on a fairly busy street in the '50s, we had a lovely, large porch. I would often sit on the top step and lean against the stone pillar and say hello to people walking by or wave to the cars going up and down the street if I knew them. Sometimes they beeped "hello." As a teenager, I waited on the porch for a boyfriend to pull his car up in front of the house.

I think that the world changed dramatically when the front porch became the back patio, and we all hid behind our houses instead of sitting and interacting with the world as it passed in front of our eyes.

Our porch had two Adirondack chairs that were used mostly by me during lazy summer days, although my father often sat reading his evening paper there after work. I hardly ever remember my mother sitting on the porch. Aren't mothers always too busy to sit?

I sat for hours with a good book, feet propped on the railing. The porch was four steps high and not far from the sidewalk. When I became engaged to Jim, who was an electrician, my mother asked if he would wire the jockey sitting on top of the heavy stone column. The jockey in his black boots and red jacket held a lantern—maybe you've seen one like it. Jim had to crawl under the porch to hammer a hole through the cement wall into the basement so that he could run the wire that would light our jockey's lamp.

I still live in the same town, pretty far from this house where I grew up, but I occasionally drive past it. In the darkness it's nice to see the light on over the steps and know that my fiancé broke his back putting that light in so many years ago.

Both my parents are gone and now my husband of forty-eight years has died, but the light he installed still shines as bright as when he installed it in 1958.

Another porch I loved was just down the same street, where my maternal grandparents owned a two-family house. We lived on the first floor until I was seven.

My brother and I would often play on the second-floor porch. We turned over huge rocking chairs to make a fort, with tablecloths shielding us from unwanted eyes and enemies. We would sit for hours watching the traffic on the busy cross street, a few houses away.

My father's parents also lived on the same street, down near the park we played in and watched baseball games. My father had fallen in love with my mother when he saw her walking by his house to her job each day.

In the early '40s, my parents bought a house on the same street. Italian families in those days stayed close. The house we bought "up the hill" had three bedrooms, one bathroom, and the great porch.

Do you think the suburbs are a failure because no one is ever on the green lawns? No one ever yells "Hi" to passing people who are not actually there because no one walks on the sidewalk anymore—well, sometimes children coming from school, but not much. The '40s and '50s were a friendlier time, right?

I often wonder about the SLOW sign I see on a road I travel frequently. Slow for what? No one is ever outside anymore. I deliberately speed up when I see that sign. Maybe someday I will have to pay for not going slow enough. Maybe I'll see children playing on their immaculate lawns. Maybe any houses with big porches will look friendly as I whiz by in my car. Maybe.

Young Years (1956 – 1980)

Xmas 1956

Along Came Love

I can still remember the first time I saw Jim. He was walking on the beach. I had just turned twenty-one, was a new college graduate, and would be starting my first teaching job in the fall. I was sitting in my black bathing suit (so he remembered), and I watched this man/boy walking along the shoreline carrying a football in his arm, as though he knew what he was doing and where he was going. What went through my mind, because he was built like an Adonis, was *what a hunk of man that is.* I thought he probably played football for some big college like Michigan State. He looked how a college football player was supposed to look.

He actually was planning to play a game of touch football on the beach with some of the guys I knew pretty well. He spotted me and asked one of them to introduce us. Harry came to where I sat and said, "Arlene, I want you to meet Jim McCarren. Jim, this is Arlene Costantin."

When Harry left, he sat down on his football, and I said, patting a spot near me, "Do you want to sit on the blanket?"

He surprised me by saying "No thanks."

Every other boy I ever knew would have said "Sure." *This one thinks for himself.*

Eight of us girls were staying at a beach house, and these same guys came every night for dinner. We all waitressed and most of the boys were lifeguards. All of us chipped in money for food and rent. Jim said he had been out drinking the night before with these guys, hometown friends. They had all agreed to play touch football on the beach in the morning.

Suddenly he said, "I haven't had breakfast yet," and I responded, brazen girl that I was, "I'll walk with you if you buy me a cup of coffee," and he said "Okay."

As we were walking, he asked if I knew anywhere he could eat. I told him he could come back to the house and I would either cook him a breakfast, or give him coffee, or some such thing.

At the house I ran upstairs to comb my hair and check myself in a mirror. I left him in the kitchen talking with a girl he knew.

My parents would often visit me, taking me out to eat, or if my mother brought down her homemade lasagna, we would share it with whoever was around. When I came downstairs, my mom and dad were talking to this boy I had just met. I introduced him to my parents, and since Barbara was there and he knew her from home, I said goodbye and that I would be spending the day with my mother and father.

I spent all day thinking of him, wondering if he and I would get together. My mother said she thought he was a man (as opposed to the "boys" I had been dating) and that she was surprised he was my friend, not Barbara's date. Later, I learned that he was twenty-five, and I realized he was the oldest guy I had ever dated. Until then, my dates had been my age.

When my parents dropped me off later that afternoon, Harry's girlfriend said that this boy Jim had come by twice to see if I was back yet. I felt excited.

Jim came back about five o'clock and invited me out for an evening. I was afraid to say yes and go with him alone since I didn't know him at all. He said the guys were planning a party at their place and there would be a lot of people I knew. So I went.

That first date was the start of a fifty-year relationship. I have nice memories of us laughing at the front door when he would be dropping me off at two o'clock in the morning after the bars had closed. The next day the girls would yell at me, or not waiting, they just yelled out the window to "SHUT UP!"

I often think we knew each other in a past life and were meant to be together again. He was a faithful, Irish Catholic man. I had read somewhere that Irish men make the best husbands and lovers and, maybe, that influenced me to marry him.

But that would not happen for quite a while since there would be the event that would alter my life.

Christmas Gift

Jim had been engaged to a girl when he was in the Army and had broken up with her. He told me he had surprised her with an engagement ring.

It was our first Christmas together. We were very much in love and had spent such close quality time for weeks together at the shore. So, as Christmas was approaching, for some outlandish reason, I began to think that he was going to surprise me with an engagement ring. Jim had introduced me to a men's store so I went there to buy him a wool sweater for Christmas. But how would a sweater compare to a diamond ring?

I was very nervous, feeling much anxiety. When Christmas came, he gave me Chanel N°5!

When we became engaged months later, no surprise. He chose the ring in a solitaire setting that I wanted. It was a small flawless diamond. I wear it to this day.

Our First Apartment

DePaul is a thriving Catholic high school in Wayne, New Jersey. Jim established a football program there because he knew that boys would not go to the new school if it did not have a football team.

Jim started the football program and was its first coach. On his own, with the permission of the Director of the school, Father McHugh, he solicited money from businessmen he knew and from all the bars he had frequented—being the good, strong, Irish drinker that he was. He outfitted an entire team with practice and game uniforms and with the equipment needed: goalposts, footballs, and so forth

Everyone seemed to want the football team at the brand new high school. There were only three-year students; it did not yet have a senior class, but that did not stop Jim. Father McHugh liked Jim, as did the nun principal.

The architects had designed a small but efficient apartment for the priest director. However, Father McHugh chose to live in a house close to the school. Jim and I were also having a house built. We had put a healthy deposit down and expected it to be completed by the time we were married in July. It was not to be. The house would not be ready for occupancy until September or October. When Father found out that our house would not be ready for us, he offered us the apartment in the school, free of charge.

My memories of that long ago time are many. I cooked my first meal—broiled chicken legs—from a wedding gift. It was Betty Crocker's cookbook. I felt very proud of taking up my married duties, though I thought mopping the small linoleum floor seemed like such hard work. The apartment had a sitting room, kitchen, bathroom, and bedroom. We were alone when we first moved to the school in August, but when the students arrived in September, it was busy with people.

Jim loved setting up football things and meeting the boys who came out for first day of practice. One time, a strange sight greeted the football squad—I had forgotten to remove the wash from the line hanging between the goalposts. Jim was not pleased!

In the fall, Jim cut the tendon in his thumb badly and so could not work for a few weeks. I was teaching school in Clifton. I would drive up the long driveway in the morning on the way to work and Jim would be standing at the door waving to me. I remember him sneaking ice cream out of the cafeteria at night.

I was also the school's first cheerleading coach and taught the girls all the cheers I remembered from my own high school cheering days. In the 1960 yearbook, there is a picture of our first daughter being taken care of by girls while I coached. Father often said if they ever bought the corn field next to the school, they would name it McCarren Field. It was not to be.

We were able to visit our house, which was taking its time being finished. But it was beautiful and large—three bedrooms, two-and-a-half bathrooms, and a two-car garage. In the '60s, this house cost $24,000!

Those were interesting and unique times for us. Jim had been an All-State high school football player from Pompton Lakes, New Jersey, and he always loved coaching.

Many Births

The birth of our first daughter and how hard it was remains a vivid memory for me. The doctor had me come to the hospital at about one o'clock in the afternoon on June 2, and she was born early morning on June 3.

In those days the husband was only allowed to visit at regular hours, and so I lay in the hospital bed and sweated through the labor pains by myself. When Jim did visit, I walked the halls with him, once in the afternoon and once in the evening. The doctor told him to go home and he would be called when the birth started.

I remember the doctor breaking my water to make the contractions stronger. I don't know if it worked. I only remember walking the halls. People did not seem so concerned about infection in those days. Didn't we all seem a lot healthier?

I lay in the bed in a ward and heard other women screaming and moaning. It was horrible for me and very frightening. Would I die delivering my baby? When the pains started, I was so overwrought a nurse told me to relax.

At 1:30 a.m. on June 3, I began having heavier contractions. The doctor gave me medication that knocked me out. I have no memory of the actual birth—the pain, the fear, and the noise. The doctor had to use forceps to help the baby emerge, and he was proud that there was not a mark on her head. When I woke from unconsciousness, the room was quiet, and as I put my hand on my stomach, I knew that my baby had been born. I had a flat stomach!

They brought Katherine Anne to me so I could see and hold her. I told them I was planning to nurse. This was 1960 and nursing babies was rare. One nurse said, "There's not much of a nipple there. She'll have to make one." Today, she'd probably be fired for that remark if I complained.

I became pregnant with my second child almost immediately. Because I experienced all the pains yet was unconscious during the birth of my first child, I chose to stay home until the last possible minute.

Looking back now it's a funny story. My husband's and father's birthdays were a day apart at the end of July. We invited my parents and my in-laws, including my husband's younger brother, to our home for a birthday celebration. We were sitting on our lovely, screened porch when I felt the first little contraction. I was already two weeks past my due date and I decided to go up to our bedroom.

"Yeah, go lie down. We're fine," they all said.

I could hear them laughing and enjoying each other from the open bathroom window.

I was starting more serious labor so I hollered "Jim." Nothing.

A little louder, "Jim." The talking and laughing below continued.

A third time, "Jim," as loud as I thought I could scream.

When I waited and still did not hear any interruption in their frivolity, I let it rip. "JIM!"

I was feeling furious. How could I be so ignored?

This time he heard me, and when he came to the bedroom door, I told him it was time for us to go. We arrived at the hospital at 11:40 p.m. My husband told our doctor that there was an extra fifty dollars in it for him if the baby was born by midnight. Peg, our second daughter, was born at 12:20 a.m. on July 27. So her grandpa would share the same birthday instead of her father! That became a source of family banter and teasing. But I had a very fast delivery and remembered most of it.

After that birth I wanted to be fully awake when my babies came through me. There were beginnings of rumblings about natural childbirth—Grantly Dick-Reade, a male obstetrician, had written the book *Childbirth Without Fear.* So almost two years later when I was pregnant again, I read this book. My doctor didn't care if I wanted a natural birth; that was my business.

So our third daughter, Alice, was born with my feeling all the pains, especially as her head came out. And as soon as her head came out, I felt a great relief. Some people say the shoulders are tough. They don't know what they are talking about! Once the head passes through that small opening, the pain is basically over.

Jim and I went on to have a fourth daughter, Jeanne. This time I had a spinal. When my funny husband visited me, he said, "What happens if there's a fire?" because I was paralyzed from the waist down. But I was able to watch her birth with no pain at all! Just seeing all that black hair crowning was sensational. I knew it was happening to me but was so detached that it looked like a television documentary.

For our fifth child, I was again late arriving at the hospital. We stopped for coffee at a drive-through when the contractions had momentarily stopped. I had no fear of delivering in the car. What was I thinking? I mostly remember sitting on the toilet at the hospital, not knowing if the baby or my bowels were coming. I felt a lot of pain and fear.

It was a boy! Welcome, James Joseph IV.

My child-bearing years were happy, hectic times. Busy, busy, busy. I found a helpful woman in Brooklyn experienced in nursing technique and nursed all my children for four months.

Now these same daughters and my daughter-in-law nurse their babies for a year or two. Imagine that! I was ahead of my time.

The Kiss

When my husband was sent on a business trip for three months, he wanted me to go with him. I would not leave our five children for such a long time. The oldest was twelve and the youngest, seven. But, after my parents offered to stay with them, we decided I could visit with Jim for ten days. Since he was traveling around the world—starting in Ireland, going into England, Germany, France, and Italy—the plan was to meet in Paris and to sightsee both Paris and Rome.

It was my first visit to Paris and much of my memory of this trip has faded. Jim claimed we ate at the top of the Eiffel Tower; I don't remember. We did visit the Coliseum in Rome and saw the catacombs.

I do remember some great meals, especially in Paris where we asked our hotel concierge to recommend a restaurant in walking distance. It was one of the better meals of the trip!

I also had a good time at home while he was gone because my parents were terrific. My dad liked driving and seeing places, and so we often all piled into our station wagon and saw sights; the Gingerbread Castle comes to mind. This was a marvelous attraction that I had seen as a kid myself, and taking my own children there was a treat. Sadly, it was dismantled sometime in the late '80s.

But my most cherished memory is of meeting Jim in the Paris airport. My husband and I had never been separated other than an occasional weekend when I would go on a retreat or Jim would have a business weekend in Maine or Florida. So the separation of six weeks was difficult for us.

At the airport, I left the plane and walked to the area where we had agreed to meet. He had given me very specific instructions. When I saw him, he looked magnificent: clean shaven, slim, and handsome. I am not sure what he saw when he spotted me, but we ran towards each other.

The kiss we shared was remarkable. We stood there hugging and kissing for quite a while and what flashed through my mind were cameras swooshing around us. We were in a scene for a movie in Paris: cameras rolling, spinning the way they do around two people kissing passionately. It was thrilling for me. We loved one another and had been apart for a long time.

We both enjoyed the city for a few days and had even more fun in Rome.

Yet what I remember most of my whole trip was that kiss.

Learning To Drive

I taught most of our children how to drive. I'm sure Jim pitched in when he could, but most of the time I was the one in the passenger seat holding on for dear life; we did not have seat belts in those days. Kathy, our oldest, was driving too far and for too long when she made a right-hand turn and scraped the fender. She was heart-broken, but I was the guilty one because she was only learning; I kept her out too long and she became tired.

I recall another incident when our second daughter Peg was learning. She was on a quiet, neighboring street and jammed on the brakes. When I asked her why—there were no cars or people around—she said, "I didn't want to hit the bird in the road."

I told her, "If you ever hit a bird, I will give you five hundred dollars!"

We laugh about that today because she has said she would often speed up trying to hit a bird. So although my logic made sense in order to teach her about braking, I did not expect that one day she might have an accident racing to hit a bird to earn five hundred dollars!

I do not have any memories of our other three children, Alice, Jeanne, and Jimmy, doing anything really unusual. Once one of them took a wide swing left in order to turn right into our driveway and a car hit us. It is a natural instinct in new drivers to swing wide, I think.

I'm reminded of when I was a new driver and backed out of our driveway and smashed into a car parked directly across the street. I took off quickly, parked at a White Castle up the street, and called home.

The phone was ringing and my dad answered. The conversation from over fifty years ago is burned in my memory.

Me: "Hi, Dad." (Fearful of telling him what I had done)

Dad: "We know. Come home."

The car belonged to a neighbor's friend, and he agreed to say that my father was the one driving to help with the insurance claim.

1974 at the Jersey Shore

A young life has been snuffed out—an ocean drowning! I did not know her, but she has touched me. I will be perceptually changed because of this knowledge, because of this pain. I feel so for the mother—with her joy and pleasure of vacation, of the beach and the ocean, of the easy living, and now? She will ask why. She will ask what if.

And I think in this moment, if I could bear some of the horror, some small part of her grief, I would help it disappear from her. Maybe that's what prayer is.

Why do we have to bear such grief when the sun is so warm, so intimate on the sand, so nurturing? When the breeze touches the clothes hanging on the line so gently, so completely, and I feel me—the joy in me? And, suddenly, I am afraid that my loves will somehow be punished because I am allowed so much happiness, so much joy in life.

I learned when young, through my church, that grief was some kind of test. For what? Who tests? What happens if you pass? Or if you fail? Horror upon horror awaits you.

But there is no failure. There's living and there's dying. So I weep for that beautiful young life erased too quickly, too soon.

And I mostly weep for the family remaining. Does my weeping or praying mean anything, anything at all?

Life Moves On (1980 – 2000)

Caught!

A friend is telling a story about being busted by New York police because he is wearing a police jacket, borrowed from a friend. His telling me reminds me of a funny story of my own. It's not really funny; it's rather strange actually.

I am approaching the Lincoln Tunnel on my way to an appointment in the city. A huge truck is in front of me, and as it slowly moves away and I pull up to the toll person, she says, "I'm closed!" She is sitting counting dollar bills.

I start to fume. What do you mean closed? I can't back up: there are cars behind me; some are shifting to move to other lanes. I did not see the red light go on because of the massive truck.

She calls a security guard over. This is ridiculous! I am so innocent about what is happening that I wave him over, too. She tells him I am abusing her; when I tell my side, he calls another policeman over to us.

I decide to take off. This is not working for me and I have to be in the city soon. As I am racing from the toll booth, I see two police cars beginning to drive towards the tunnel, and here's the funny part, I think, "Wow, they must be chasing some drug runner, really bad guy," and then they stop their cars in front of me, blocking me from moving. These cars are for me? How is this happening?

One officer yanks me from my car, hurting my wrist. I am suddenly frightened and tell him to TAKE IT EASY.

They look at my driver's license and registration and give me a citation to appear in court. A daughter says she will go with me but I am still so cocky and confident that I go alone.

When I tell the judge what happened, she believes the police officer and says that she sees no reason for him to lie and fines me court costs, which I think are not so bad.

It is only later that I learn that our insurance rates will climb, and points are not removed for three years.

I am a criminal for trying to run the Lincoln Tunnel.

My impatience and anger cost me a lot of money, unfairly I still think. I am sure if I had waited the toll person out, she would have finished counting her money and taken my four dollars. A hard and expensive lesson learned.

Food Experiences

Another vivid memory is Jim's and my visit to the Au Tunnel restaurant in New York City. I ordered tripe, an interesting and somewhat unique Italian dish. It was one of the most delicious meals I ever ate, and I suppose it was partly due to the fact that Jim and I were in love and lust (again). We were both in our fifties.

I sat with my back against the wall and Jim sat to my right. The crock filled with the tripe was put to my left and I could either help myself to the magnificent, pungent dish to satisfy my intense food hunger or let the waiter serve me. He would spring over whenever I lifted the lid.

This memory makes me think about our dining experiences in Paris when I went to visit Jim. Are there any other great cities in which to eat?

I don't remember any food we ate, but I do recall strongly that, when we ordered dessert, our waiter recommended a bottle of wine, and we decided to try it. This was a first for us. A separate wine? Just for our dessert?

I can still remember what a true match it was. I was blown away at how the wine and dessert complimented each other so that their tastes subtly exploded in my mouth. For the first time

I understood why some people become wine connoisseurs. They know how to choose the exquisitely correct wine with any food.

One other marvelous meal I remember was in 1994 when Jim and I visited the village in Northern Italy where my maternal grandparents were born. I still have second and third cousins there.

We stayed at a beautiful Swiss-style chalet under three magnificent mountains. Cortina, where the Winter Olympics were held years ago, is half-an-hour away.

One cousin, Anna, cooked us a risotto with mushrooms and small pieces of many vegetables and onions—a truly unique taste and experience.

Working for Jamie

I saw a Shiatsu lady in the '80s. She was wonderful with me, and I enjoyed the massages very much. During my first massage, I *saw* the Virgin Mary standing like her statues show her: arms open and inviting. I knew she was in my mind, and I said, "I see Mary." Jamie responded, "She's your sister."

I also had two more unique experiences. Jamie must have pressed the right points because I felt myself sliding off a tree (I was an ape/monkey) and into the earth and being covered with soil. It was not scary; it was a gift to me so that I could understand that we come from the earth, that evolution has created me on this planet.

The other happened as Jamie pressed certain areas. I felt myself out in the universe among the planets and stars and I said, "I hear my song. It's loud." It was blaring in my head.

She told me, "Put a white light around it."

Jamie was one of several very powerful teachers for me. When I was young and a new parent, I remember one of my children starting to hug me and want closeness, and I knew on some level that it was because my unconscious was being treated and being made open and accepting.

I sought and learned from all these teachers, including my children, parents, and husband.

Jamie opened a gem store, and she asked me if I wanted to work in it. I worked in the back, with bookkeeping kinds of chores: listing the incoming units and organizing merchandise. Some young yuppies would come and just stand in the store, looking, and I often got the feeling that they were trying to pick and use the vibrations they imagined they got. Maybe there really were vibrations coming from the gems and Indian stones and artifacts that were displayed in the glass trays. I believed, also, in those days; believed that jade and quartz and opals were healing. I bought a beautiful necklace and some earrings at cost. A daughter has the necklace now.

Once I inventoried a long list and did not write any names, and Jamie called me into her office to ask , "What is this?" When I said I had no idea what the merchandise was, she frowned, upset; but she was gentle with me—angry, but gentle. I learned a lesson that day.

Jamie got close to one of my daughters. When Jamie was divorcing her Italian husband, she wanted to talk to my daughter since my daughter worked for Jamie's husband. I would not give her my daughter's phone number because I knew Jamie wanted information about her husband.

I remember the time Jamie gave her sixteen-year-old daughter a lavish party for her bat mitzvah. She invited her hair-dresser (for God's sake!) but not me. Anyway, I did think then that she was spoiling her sixteen year old.

I loved Jamie and respected what she did for me. She had talent and tried to get an acupuncture degree but left the class, which she said was too male-dominated and almost anti-female.

I have heard recently after twenty years that she is now an acupuncturist. I am happy for her. I often wonder if she ever married again. She probably did. She was a woman who liked men and enjoyed marriage, I think.

Florence

The other day I came across things I had saved from my trip to Florence, Italy, in the spring of 1997. I have a dilemma; do I throw the paper memories away or do I continue to let them clutter my spaces?

I loved the trip but it had its moments. I was often annoyed at my roommate who would wake me by turning the television on at three or four o'clock in the morning when she could not sleep. She said because she was a widow she was used to the television being on almost all the time. I forget her name but I do remember hurting her feelings once when she asked me to save her a seat at dinner and I sat at a table for four with three other friends. She was stunned and embarrassed when she walked into the dining room. I did apologize to her later.

I met Jeanne, a fellow traveler, and we became close. She invited me the next summer to Saratoga where she was vacationing with some women. In the end, I did not go since it was too hard for me to not only make the decision but also plan what I needed to do to get there by myself.

Jim was unwilling to travel much. He was able—but beginning his downward spiral into his handicap—and chose to stay home with our dog. Did he refuse because he wanted me to have some fun without him? Yes, that was part of our life together, but only in the years after he retired in 1994.

I loved Florence and felt very much like a Florentine walking through the city, wearing my jacket, acting as though I had lived there all my life and was on my way to somewhere important.

And the David! As a teenager, I had seen a special on Michelangelo and had old pamphlets and college brochures from an art class about him. The statue was so huge! I had no idea the statue would be so large. I had seen people in pictures standing at the pedestal, but I could have never imagined the impact that statue had on me. I spent an hour or more sitting, looking, walking around, seeing the beauty from every angle. I had read that the particular block of marble, from which David emerged, was rejected by other sculptors because it was inferior. And Michelangelo SAW the David in it and called him out.

It was truly splendid looking at the strong-and-angry concentrated expression in his eyes, the curved hand holding the sling, the muscles in his calves, his toenails, and his magnificent physique. This is marble? This was created by one man?

All in all, I experienced a marvelous tour of a remarkable city that is revered by many. I am one of them.

Last Sail

My brother Allan was quite the sailor. He would sail yachts from New Jersey to Florida, or the islands, for people who did not have the time or the inclination to sail the ocean. He could map the plans so that, sure enough, an ocean marker would appear exactly where he said it would and in the time prescribed, give or take a brisk wind or two.

My husband and I were experiencing a difficult time. Jim had gotten very fat. He was disappointed in his job and had become quiet, withdrawn, and not very active. He sat and watched television and had little interest in much of anything.

So a cruise was planned for four couples: Jim's younger brother and his wife; Allan and his wife Em; another husband and wife who were friends of Allan's; and Jim and me.

Small quarters but fun! We sailed the Nantucket waters, Provincetown, and the surrounding islands, Martha's Vineyard included. I do remember Jim's brother, Jack, saying he had no idea that Jim had retreated so much into himself and was losing his interest in being active. His weight was making him sit more. However, Jim did like the activities involved in sailing, the physicality of it. He had grown up on a lake and sailed as a young man.

I do like looking at the pictures we took of the trip: of the mopeds we rented to bike around the island and of a picnic lunch near the beach.

I began to feel attracted to my brother's friend. He, the man whose name I cannot remember, started flirting with me, giving me long soulful looks, and I found myself drawn to him.

I still feel the sting of hurting Jim because one night, when we were tied to a dock, this man and I, feeling our mutual attraction, walked to the end of the pier. He leaned down to kiss me. I heard a moan and, turning before we could kiss, saw Jim standing there watching us. He had followed us.

I got frightened—my Catholic background kicked in, I'm sure—making the rest of the trip strange for me. I felt awkward and guilty. I hadn't done anything but wanted to, being so lonely and angry at Jim. My brother said that this man always liked to be the ladies man and often flirted outrageously with women at parties.

Jim and I never went sailing together again. As I look back on it, I should have insisted.

About ten or fifteen years later, my brother invited me to sail alone with him, without Jim, who could not have navigated the yacht anyway. There were three yachts: two of them captained by Allan's sons with their wives and children. We sailed the Chesapeake and visited an old family friend who had a magnificent home right on the water.

I loved every minute of it! Swimming off the yacht, the fine dining and friendship with nieces and nephews, visiting Annapolis, all so good. At the end of the sail, my brother said that it had been a great time for all BECAUSE I was a part of it. I was flattered. I think I was able to contribute to the ease and peace of so many people in such close quarters. I taught two of my nieces to knit and there are great pictures showing me concentrating on their efforts.

I look back on that interesting flirtation that hurt Jim and remember having another more serious one. I was bored with Jim and his shut-down behavior. But nothing ever happened anytime I flirted with a man who responded to me, and so I never committed adultery.

Was I happy? I am not sure. It may have been fun. Who knows?

DREAM CATCHER
ROCK HALL, MD
PRIORITY

Priority
crew
STEVE

Summer Dream 1981

I had a beautiful little dream last night. It woke me. It was very short and seems important.

In my dream, there was a small vase of flowers on the kitchen table. I was looking at the flowers. They were the most beautiful flowers, in a most simple arrangement. I had to take a quick deep breath to withstand the beauty. I felt this would never be seen in real life, that the colors and brilliance of the flowers were not of the earth, that they were symbolic, ethereal, rather than real.

As I was looking at them and beginning to wake, a voice said, "This is your life." I lay there understanding that I would be here for a very short period of time and that in the entire universe the loveliness and simplicity of the flowers stood out. The smallness of the arrangement paralleled time. I knew I would be in existence for a second of eternal time.

I also saw how beautiful my life was or was capable of being.

I thought if I truly believed it, my life would take on a beauty—a small gift, if you will, to all who know me and live in my time frame.

I also sensed that my life was a jewel. I experienced God showing me my life and what I can think of it. He was showing me how much I was loved and valued. The unique colors were other-worldly, not of this earth.

I had quit a thirty-year, three-pack-a-day smoking habit on April 11, 1981, and I often wonder if that had anything to do with this dream—a renewal of life, a wish to breathe and to be healthy and well.

Blue-White Yeager Diamond

We were engaged and Jim gave me a beautiful and perfect diamond. It was small, half a carat, and it was flawless. It was in a solitaire setting.

I was the director of a preschool for battered and disturbed children, ones whose parents were drunks or drug-addicted. One day, I had to drive my son to an interview at a New York state college. I left the school with my head teacher in charge.

I dropped my son off at the college and went to a game room on the highway to pass time. As I was driving back to the college, I spotted my diamond was missing from my ring! My hands were on the steering wheel when I noticed it. Horror and fear went through me and I experienced that *this isn't happening to me* moment. I went back to the place and a man looked all around where I had been playing; he even moved the machine. Then I walked the parking lot stopping at every little glint of aluminum foil that people discard. And I prayed, "Help me, Jesus. Help me, St. Anthony*, to find my diamond."

I wrote a poem to my diamond as my son was taking his placement tests. I sat outside on a bench in the shade of a huge tree and penned an ode. I asked that the diamond stay lost and not found because I imagined it would be abused somehow; the person finding it would not recognize its purity and magnificence.

When I got home, I called the head teacher and asked her to look for the diamond in the school. There were three classrooms and my office.

The next day, a Saturday, my phone rang. It was Dorothy, my head teacher. We chatted for a while and then she said, "Don't you want to ask about your diamond?"

I held my breath because I could not imagine that the impossible had happened.

"I found it," she said calmly.

I don't remember how I responded in my excitement and awe. Probably something like "Don't tell me. You're kidding!"

She gave me the diamond on Monday. She had wrapped it in a tissue, and there it was, sparkling in its brilliance.

She told me that she had been on the phone and was doodling as she talked. When she noticed her doodle, she saw it was a ring and it reminded her to look for my diamond. She glanced at the wooden floor boards and saw a sparkle between the boards, and sure enough, it was a diamond.

I tried to give her a gift in thanks, but she would not take it. My best friend at the school and I called her an old soul, someone who has lived on this planet before.

My husband had the ring reset and I am wearing it now as I record this memory.

I saved the doodle Dorothy made as she sat talking on the phone. I used it for years as a bookmark.

*St. Anthony spent forty years in the desert and was thought lost. When he returned to his village, he was revered as a mystic. He is often called upon to find lost things, mostly by Catholics. I thank him to this day.

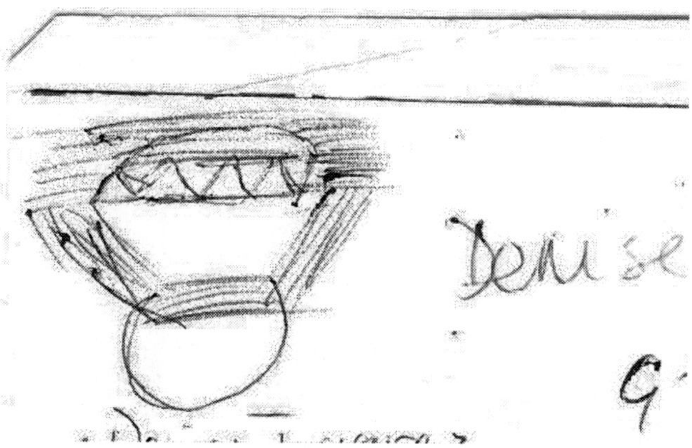

Writing as Salvation 1985

During the fall of 1985, my bipolar disorder reoccurred and I spent a week in the hospital. I had become more and more manic, after losing a great job and sitting around doing nothing all summer. But I did write a lot. What I share with you here is my personal journey of a return to sanity.

The morning of December 23, I was taken to a hospital. My brain was literally exploding, as one minute I was wrapping Christmas presents on the dining room table and the next I was in my bra and panties screaming in front of my two grown daughters and son. Minutes were lost—perhaps like sleep walking? I could hear one daughter on the phone to an old therapist. He suggested calling an ambulance, and she did. But I am getting ahead of my story. My nightmare started the night before.

What follows are notes from my writings.

Sunday, December 22, 1985

I have decided to begin writing again because there doesn't seem to be anything else I really want to do.

I imagine myself sitting quietly and peacefully inside a silent bubble while faint sounds of the world around me continue.

I have not written for a week and what a difference that makes in my life. Since these writings will be only for me, I will be able to tell you all so much.

Like right now I am sitting in the corner of my bedroom in a very comfortable chair and I hear my husband and daughter talking in the kitchen. Jim talks slow enough; I can hear his rhythm. He seems to want me to stay with his rhythm. I get frightened getting into his rhythm.

I have been losing my rhythm in the world. When I feel most intensely me, I hear huge winds whipping outside, roars far away and close, noises I recognize and some I don't. Sounds that frighten me—booms and radios—sounds of living, not of dying. I sit here listening to my insides, which are quiet, and hearing the sounds outside of my own self. And the more I sit inside myself the more confused I seem to become. Goodbye means death to me, so that the music playing right now tells me not to believe I am dead and also not to expect other people to know exactly what I want or even to know anything I really want.

I can be Toscanini; I can be Einstein. I am Toscanini; I am Einstein. I am also Arlene. I'm a 50 year old brilliant woman who is tired of pretending to be what I am not, the tiredness I feel.

How do you know when you are dead? How do you know when (or if) other people are dead?

I made doodles on the page: a house, door emphasized; arrows; trees; lines with bows through them.

Idiot scribbles. Hang on, Arlene. If I am in the Now, and there is no one with me, then what? Then I am dead, from moment to moment to moment. I cannot share myself 100% of the time.

That night, I was experiencing insanity. I sat in my bedroom while my family sat in the den watching TV. I sat with my crazy mind and did not know how to alter it or stop it. My son

Jimmy came and sat with me; he sat on the bed, facing me in my chair holding my notebook. I remember only saying to him, "Now. Now. Now." He was trying to reach me but I was gone. When Jimmy left I continued writing.

Rather than die, I choose to go into hell. I would be crazy for the world. Soul afraid of dying doesn't know how to live.

So each person goes into his little shell and says pretend words like "I'm sorry. I'll never do it again" and then expect in some future moment—5 seconds, 5 years, 50 years, 500 years, 5000 years—to be back, to be back to frightening themselves so much.

That babies come here to die—that babies come here, hell, to be abused and burned and starved and smashed—so what? If I think I am God, I've just arrived on this planet and I have to work very hard to be heard at all because it's all pretense. It's all wishing for one more chance. I don't know how to live here—I can't stay here—you bring death and destruction to yourself, over and over and over, as long as someone—oh, so beautiful, so caring, so warm, so willing, so funny—is on your FUCKING SCREEN!

Help me-help me-help me-help me-help me-help me-help me-help me

I am not the one who is insane. If you all stay outside in your TV land—you are unreal—you are again a false prophet-and I have died—inside of me—but you will never know—you don't look at me—fear—pretend—"you're crazy"—yes, I'm in here—I cannot make believe—I cannot live, not sure which world is real—the one I'm in or the one I'm watching on the TV screen.

Anything that has to be viewed on a live screen is false!

I AM:

Deep clear breaths that go past my lungs to the ground.

I AM:

Cold pictures of bears and phones and rugs and non-moving

No, Moving

I AM:

A warm pink glowing room

I do not need—I have enough air to take deep clear breaths and I can live this way for a long time

I AM:

Ice cold hands that cannot write good

I usually come here when I'm angry—enraged, really, at the world.

I may come here again. I may not.

Don't scare me, please. When I am Here, Now, I am so clear, so bright, so joyful, so okay.

You can find your own NOW.

And now-now-now heartbeat heartbeatfaster faster slow slowslowslow SHOW IS OVER

Once during the night I woke and was afraid to look in the mirror because I knew I might not see my image. I might not be here, after all. I might be dead and not know it yet. Sleepless and restless, I continued to write into the early morning hours.

Later in the day, as I was being taken out of the house, screaming on a stretcher, I remember a paramedic saying, "It's a little cold out, but it will be quick and then you'll be warm." This kind remark was the only connection I had to any reality at the time.

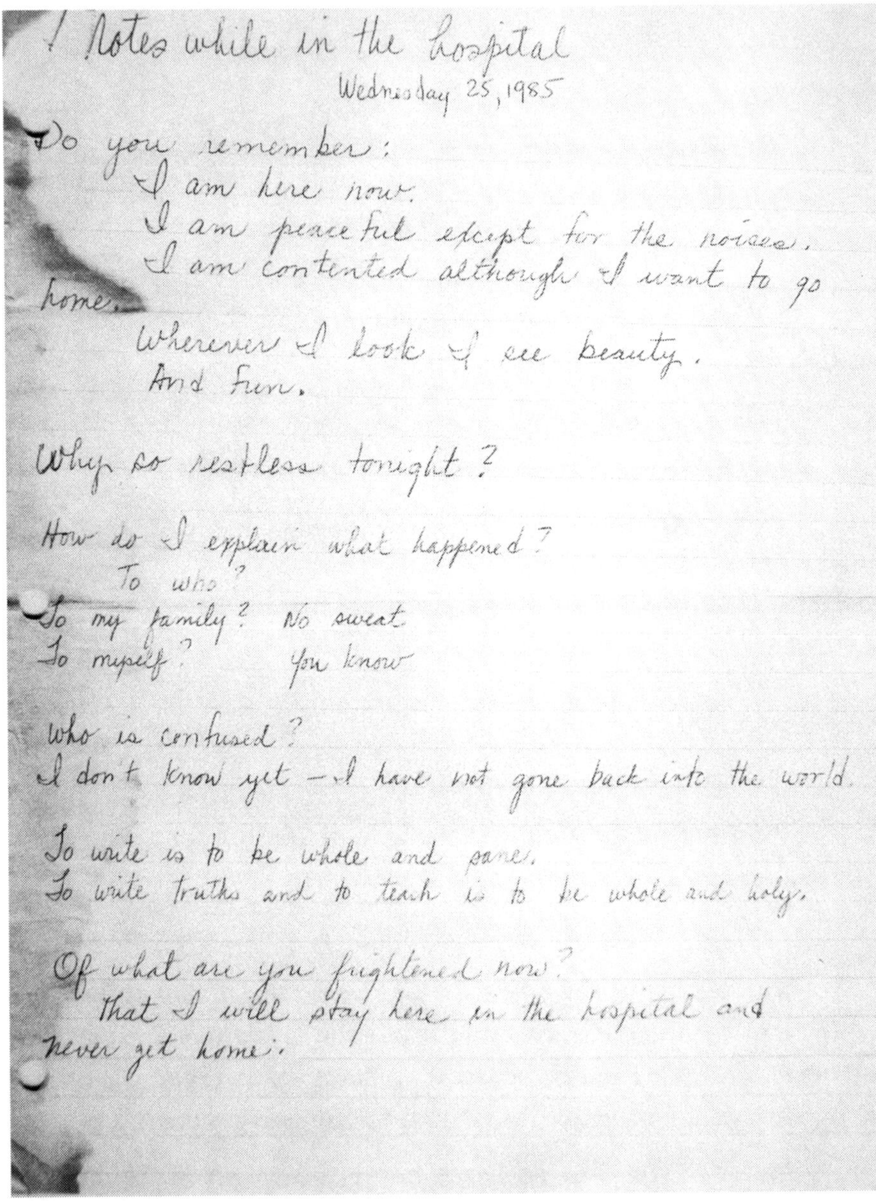
Notes while in the hospital
Wednesday 25, 1985

Do you remember:
I am here now.
I am peaceful except for the noises.
I am contented although I want to go home.
Wherever I look I see beauty.
And fun.

Why so restless tonight?

How do I explain what happened?
To who?
To my family? No sweat.
To myself? You know

Who is confused?
I don't know yet — I have not gone back into the world.

To write is to be whole and sane.
To write truths and to teach is to be whole and holy.

Of what are you frightened now?
That I will stay here in the hospital and never get home.

I wrote while I was in the hospital.

Wednesday 25, 1985

Do you remember:

I am here now

I am peaceful except for the noises

I am contented although I want to go home.

Wherever I look I see beauty. And fun.

Why so restless tonight?

How do I explain what happened?

To who?

To my family? No sweat

To myself? You know

Who is confused?

I don't know yet-I have not gone back into the world.

To write is to be whole and sane.

To write truths and to teach is to be whole and holy.

Of what are you frightened now?

That I will stay in the hospital and never get home.

I awoke at 6:15 a.m. every day. I had to shake the sleepiness and dreams from my mind and clear my eyes and mind for a new day. If I had been given medication, I found it more difficult to come awake quickly or to be consistently alert. Sounds helped to make contact with some part of me that remembered aliveness.

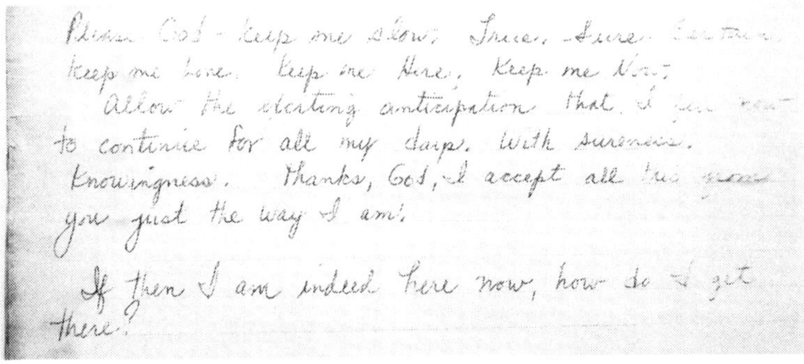

Please God - keep me slow; True, Sure, Certain.
Keep me Love. Keep me Here, Keep me Now;
Allow the exciting anticipation that I feel now
to continue for all my days. With sureness.
Knowingness. Thanks, God, I accept all this from
you just the way I am!

If then I am indeed here now, how do I get
there?

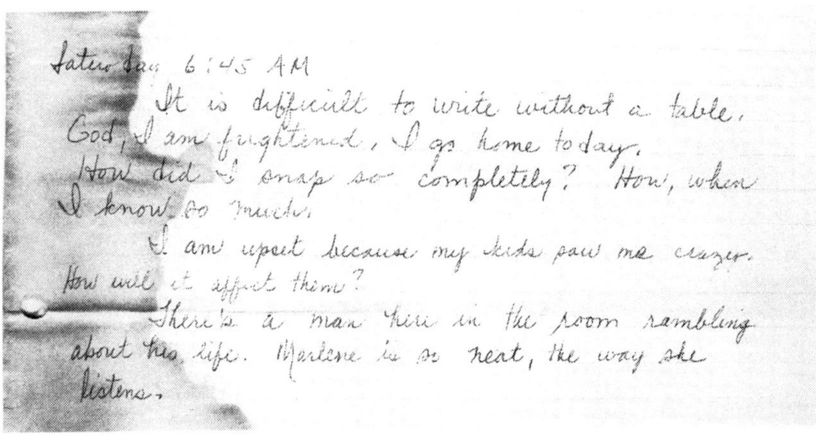

Saturday 6:45 AM
It is difficult to write without a table.
God, I am frightened, I go home today.
How did I snap so completely? How, when
I know so much.
I am upset because my kids saw me crazy.
How will it affect them?
There's a man here in the room rambling
about his life. Marlene is so neat, the way she
listens.

The sun is up and it is bright with the orange glowing light that it has as it first rises.

I wait for towels so I can bathe. Maybe I will just get dressed without bathing but I think not. I will be; I am fine as I wait for towels.

I am going home today.

I am here. I am now. Take my hand.

I will go home today, 26th of December.

What a wonderful year 1986 is going to be. It will be a year filled with joys and laughter, happiness and growth. And as 1985 ends with the sounds of the tiny baby in diapers approaching the New Year, I joyously look forward to it.

If I do not (cannot) go home today, I will be extremely angry and perturbed.

I had to stay in the hospital to get my head on straight again.

Course in Miracles: Nothing unreal exists.

Nothing real can be threatened.

Therein lies the wisdom of God.

Please God keep me slow, true, sure, certain. Keep me love. Keep me here. Keep me now.

Allow the exciting anticipation that I feel now to continue for all my days, with sureness, knowingness. Thanks, God, I accept this from you just the way I am.

If I am indeed here now, how do I get there?

My life unfolds for me to learn:

True humility, patience, truth and wisdom without fear, trust in the universe and my place in it.

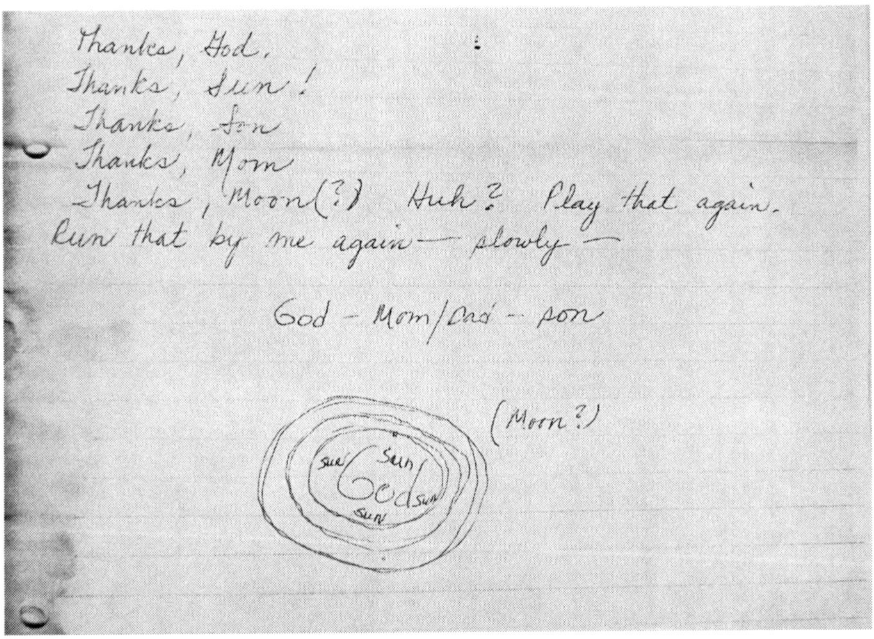
Thanks, God.
Thanks, Sun!
Thanks, Son
Thanks, Mom
Thanks, Moon(?) Huh? Play that again.
Run that by me again— slowly—

God - Mom/Dad - son

(Moon?)

sun
sun
God
sun
sun

And also my teacher, you have taught me, are teaching me what living in the now means for me. In the now I am fine. I get anxious going towards the future (where will I be in the scheme of things?) and slipping back to the past (oh, God, what happened, did I shame my children?)

Thanks, God

Thanks, Sun

Thanks, Son

Thanks, Mom

Thanks, Moon

I feel so beautiful-like I'm in exactly the body I want, with the exact sounds and thoughts I would have if I could make my wishes come true. Amen—yes—yes—

After supper on Thursday I wrote.

I sit here and set it up like a desk, an office, and wanting to write, so desperately to write. And I wonder about the ability to write experiences; the impossibility of being able to do that. For even as I record I am focused in the past, even if only two seconds or two minutes.

Crack up: Monday

Tuesday (conscious unsure what day)

Wednesday - Christmas (here first day fully aware)

Thursday (want to go home)

So, what happened? Did I collapse completely and have to be tied into a stretcher and taken to St. Joe's? Did I frighten the kids? For what purpose was that performance given? Was it on Monday? Jim kept saying wrap the presents. And what about hearing on the radio about presence rather than presents?

What day did I come here?

What day did I come here?

Oh Babes of mine, what did I do? What did I do? Alice on the phone, was she in terror, watching, wanting to help. And Jimmy & Jeannie there too. What did I do? Will you forgive? Forget?

Oh Babes, what did I do?

Friday 6:45

Again, it's the ecstacy of knowing. In sleep of kissing the sun, being completely synchronized with everything. Breathing and hearing must be together _exactly_ because waking _identifies_ the universe, the wholeness of all and the accuracy, the exquisite rightness of _my_ place; of my being here.

Again, it's the ecstacy of knowing.

God, be with me. Spirit, stay here with me and in me. I am here in a hospital, facing the fact that I had a "breakdown." God, I really am here. And what will be the repercussions? And what did my beautiful children see?

If I am indeed here, how do I get there?

What happened to me? I cleaned out the laundry room and was happy with the spaces I was making. How did I let this happen to me that I am here in a hospital?

What day did I come here?

Oh Babes of mine, what did I do? What did I do? Alice on the phone, was she in terror, watching, wanting to help. And Jimmy & Jeannie there too. What did I do? Will you forgive? Forget?

Oh Babes,what did I do?

Friday 6:45

Again, it's the ecstasy of knowing. In sleep, kissing the sun, being completely synchronized with everything. Breathing and hearing must be together exactly because waking identifies the universe, the wholeness of all and the accuracy, the exquisite rightness of my place; of my being here. Falling back into sleep into the darkness again is perfection. So that when the overhead light goes on—explosion—eyes and mind are instantly alert.

Friday 9:12 AM

SO it is all synchronicity. And I will be here today and tomorrow the doctor will meet with me and Jim and whatever kids want to come.

I cannot write of Jim yet—too nervous-making for me, to write the TRUTH of Jim and me. I do not want to now. Later I will.

Can't write it while it's happening.

Does Jim have to know? How to teach him?

Saturday 6:45 AM

It is difficult to write without a table. God, I am frightened. I go home today. How did I snap so completely? How?

I am upset because my kids saw me crazy. How will it affect them?

8:21 I have taken a bath... waiting for breakfast—going home.

And so I breathe in and out and know my aliveness and hear pleasant and familiar sounds I had come to love and know, the sounds of shoes walking down the hall, voices screaming, yelling, laughing. The quiet sounds. All the joys of Christmas come back for kids.

And I will flow with the rhythm of my life. I will teach. I will heal. I will know love. My life is filled with abundance.

I get confused sometimes. I am anxious though to resume my life outside of this hospital and to accept my life with love and perform it with grace.

I was released from the hospital on December 30. I continued to write in my journals.

I want to work. I want to weigh 150.

I am dressed now in my pretty red smock blouse and black skirt waiting at 11:15 AM to go to my brother's for a holiday celebration.

What happened to me?

I think some of us walk the brink, the edge all our lives, I believe I do, the edge of real. The edge of saintliness, the edge of passionate longing, desires, will, the will to live, to experience all that life has to offer. Sometimes it is painful, sometimes ecstatic.

ENOUGH!

When I had my first breakdown at twenty-one, I experienced my brain burning, being singed by the insanity that was taking me over. I know now that neurons were moving too swiftly across the synapses in my brain so that I literally smelled burning coming from inside me. My brain cells were being bombarded by hormones run amuck.

I believe my premenopausal hormones caused my second manic episode when I was fifty. Now, being in menopause has calmed my hormones. Bipolar disorder no longer affects me as it once did. Alleluia!

Nothing Matters

Nothing matters. Nothing really matters—not priests, religious, governors, even presidents. Nothing matters but CARE of family and friends.

Care of self is first so that others will notice how happy and healthy you are, even as you age. Aging well is often hard in this culture. Care of self is stressful for some people for they are used to caring for others and only as an afterthought to themselves. And often caring lovingly for self means doing those sometimes difficult things, like exercising all the time, even when one does not feel like it, and eating healthy foods, even when the junk foods look so appealing and are often craved!

It's important to smile or sing when the mood is low. Singing lifts the spirit and calms the soul.

Then there are the things that need to be discarded; no one knows their value except you. Yet, you hang on to these things because you feel that when you throw away the napkins that were brought back from Italy, you will be punished by your own mind. *They were very valuable, handmade, and you put them in the garbage?* And your mind will wonder how you can be so cold-hearted, destroying something so beautiful. And the worst—you will remember the napkins the rest of your life and be sorry that you could not or did not use them. You did use the matching, beautiful tablecloth every Easter. Everyone always said how beautiful and alpine-looking the set was.

Then there are all the pictures, so many—some from when you were a girl. Who will want them? You saved things because you are sentimental, like the old picture of your father that you pressed into your scrapbook when you were in high school. Why didn't my mother save it? It showed him receiving a football for winning the championship of his district. He is so young-looking, so handsome, so vulnerable. How could he know then that having sex with your mother would change the rest of his life when she got pregnant and they had to get married?

This only seems to matter to me. I often look at things and wonder about my own death and my children looking at the same items I gaze at now and saying, "Why did Mom save this? What was that about?"

Maybe one will answer, "Mom loved this picture, this ceramic, this music box because it was Grandma's or Uncle Allan's or her Nauna's. It is old and has emotional value, maybe monetary value. She was sentimental."

What about the reams and reams of papers? Old high school essays from my creative writing classes, poetry written from the early '60s when my babies were being born. My newer journals—will anyone read them or will they be burned or worse, shredded?

Covers, blankets, books, knitting magazines, more books, and more papers! What? And then there is the furniture: my mother's dining room set complete with chandelier, my mother's desk. The lamps in the bedroom were my mother-in-law's living room lamps.

Sometimes I think that the bigger the house, the more accumulated stuff. Downsizing is hard but I am determined to do it.

Irma

In 1987 my mother, dad, and aunt came to our house for our usual Thanksgiving dinner. As she was walking into the kitchen, I noticed that my mother's face was ashen and gray. What went through my mind was *Mom looks awful.* A few minutes later, after I had greeted and kissed my aunt and my dad, her complexion was fine, rosy-cheeked as usual. I thought I probably imagined what I had seen.

We had a fun and good time together. There were fourteen of us: children and future sons-in-law. I took lots of pictures. Mom is laughing in a lot of them.

My dad found a gold necklace in his pocket, and when he held it up, Mom said, "That's mine," and we helped her put it around her neck. I knew it probably belonged to their granddaughter, my brother's child, whom they had recently visited, but I said nothing.

When the dishes were done and I was looking forward to relaxing and chatting, my mother, who always had the disconcerting habit of leaving places fast, said they were going home. She lived five minutes from us.

I was annoyed but it was decided that the three of them would go. I said, "Boy, I'm not inviting you next year."

My son helped her and my aunt on with their coats.

I hugged and kissed them goodbye. As our tradition, I said "I love you" to her as I hugged her.

Later I was washing up when Jim said that my dad had called to say that mom had fainted. I was not going to go, I was so tired, but something made me get in the car with Jim to drive over there. As we rounded the corner of their dead-end street, the flashing red lights of a paramedics' vehicle stunned me. *This is more serious than fainting.*

In the living room were six or seven people pounding on her chest. Her eyes were open, unseeing. One of her breasts was exposed, and it was full and lovely. I had never seen my mother naked. No one paid attention. They kept pounding her.

She didn't revive.

I hope she had died instantly when she dropped to the floor in their small bathroom, and my dad couldn't push the door open to get to her body.

The paramedics drove slowly to the hospital where a doctor could pronounce my mother dead. I drove my dad following behind them. My husband stayed to lock up their house.

In the hospital, I closed her eyes and, from her neck, removed the gold necklace she had been so happy to receive only hours before. I am wearing the necklace as I write this. Someday a granddaughter will wear it.

After my mother's death, I hesitated developing my pictures. It seemed eerie. The pictures are wonderful because she is smiling and laughing in a lot of them. Her last day was spent with all of us, happy to be with her husband, sister, daughter and family.

Looking at the pictures, I remembered what I had seen on her face as she came into the house: her pallor, her grayness, her coming heart attack. I like to think I saw her death mask.

The Broken Chair

I often blamed myself when my husband began weighing over four hundred pounds. Once in a restaurant he sat in a chair, and it broke. He was not hurt, and they rushed to bring another chair to him. I still remember my embarrassment at his obesity. *Will this one break too?* I was ashamed being seen with him. *Why doesn't she cook better for him?*

I did not have the courage to leave the marriage and get on with a more active life. I began thinking that life sucks and then you die.

I know the need for excess food stems from anger and hopeless feelings. I tend to overeat myself when I am stressed, angry, even enraged at my lot in life right now.

Is this the end days? Last time the end was by fire; someone said this time the end days will be by water. Is this the end time for me? For Jim?

My Food Addiction

In 1987 I weighed almost two hundred pounds, and having a small frame, I looked massive. Frustrated with the many diets where I lost pounds then gained pounds then lost pounds again, I decided to join an organization that I had heard only good things about. The organization is Overeaters Anonymous and I attended my first meeting on October 21, 1987. People who are recovering alcoholics or food addicts always remember the date of their first meeting.

Overeaters Anonymous is a twelve step program that uses the steps of Alcoholics Anonymous. In its first step, AA says: "We admitted we were powerless over alcohol—that our lives had become unmanageable." OA says instead: "We admitted we were powerless over food—that our lives had become unmanageable."

I quickly got a sponsor who led me through the first five steps. I called her every day, as the program suggests. The program also suggests calling three other people every day, which I did. If I had to leave a message, I was taught to say, "Hi, this is Arlene. I'm making a call. Have a good day."

Sometimes people were home, and then I talked to them about food issues or just chatted. I started on the Weight Watchers plan and went from a size eighteen to a size eight in six months! I was able to maintain the size eight for over five years.

I am heavier now than I would like to be. Age has lessened my desire to be slim, but I still want to be healthy. I have even gone to AA meetings to listen. I go now only once a week to OA meetings, but I still practice the steps. They give a foundation for living.

Two of my grown children are also involved in a twelve step program and it gives us a platform to communicate. “Have you been to a meeting lately?” is a favorite expression we use when one of us is acting weird.

I will always love and appreciate the twelve step program and the people who live their lives using its principles.

Headlight

There was a light inside my head a long while ago in the late ‘80s, early ‘90s. It would fill the space inside my head, and I would hold my breath so that it would stay longer. Of course I believed I was special and holy.

It happened three or four times between 1987 and 1992. Once in my journal I wrote, “The light came this morning.”

I mentioned it hesitantly to two people. One was a Catholic nun. She said “Yes, yes” and dismissed it (and me). She didn’t want to talk about it, but she said she had experienced it also. There seems to be a superstitious fear in Catholics and other Christians that if you talk about something you are bragging, or it may go away, never to come back. Somehow you will be punished for having talked about it. Keep it secret. It may drive you nuts, but that’s okay. That’s the way God wants it.

Who is kidding who here?

Can it really offend God who, being God, cannot be offended? Is the light from God or from some inner-body workings? IF we keep it mysterious, are we more special?

If God doesn’t allow me to find out, investigate, seek answers, then God does not exist for me. What else can God be but the One who encourages curiosity, the One who says ”Seek,” the One who says ”Ask,” the One who says ”Find out”?

I ignored that particular nun. I wasn't courageous enough at that time in my life to pursue it with HER! She is somewhat of a tight conservative, and that is not my taste for living. I began to consider her stupid and unworthy of my attention. There would be other seekers like me. I would find them.

The other person I mentioned it to was a woman I worked with in the preschool for abused kids. She was Hispanic, the social worker who went into the children's homes, and we were good friends. When I told her of my experience, she understood immediately and shared that she had had the same experience quite often. She thought that sometimes when the body is pretty pure and clear—no junk food, some meditation—the light shines upward from within. There is no junk clogging the system. She didn't make much of it and was very casual and accepting. She helped me not to dramatize the event. We experience and then we move on.

As I write this memory, I am sorry that the light does not fill my head anymore. I am not meditating regularly; I am consuming lots of junk food; I have gained much weight; and I am angry at my circumstances right now. I am now not good enough?

I wonder sometimes about it. I like to think I was acting especially saintly then, taking care of abused children with cigarette burns hidden on their legs, and that God was filling me with his light to help me understand how truly loved I am.

I miss it. Maybe someday it will return and fill the inside of my head. Until then, I wait and work.

Me, A Chaplain?

In the late '80s and early '90s, I was accepted into a seminary school. I loved my first class on the early Christians. I wanted to learn about those first few years after Christ. He certainly influenced them so that the first writings about him were fifty years after his death.

I took many courses, commuting one day a week to New Brunswick, New Jersey, where the school was located. When I enrolled in the Pastoral Care program, I was told to go to Clara Maass Hospital in Belleville, New Jersey, and take the program there to become certified in Pastoral Care counseling.

When I interviewed with the very Catholic nun who was in charge of the internship, she said that when I had completed the program I could become a chaplain! I remember how I cried. Me? Chaplains were men in the Second World War. It was like being a priest.

The program involved seven of us and we would meet once or twice a week to discuss our work. We wrote patient evaluations on what we had done or not done. These verbatims involved dialogue: what I said, how the patient responded. They were critiqued by the supervisor (the nun) and by my colleagues. It was a tough, learning time.

I walked around visiting people with a badge that had my name and the title CHAPLAIN. A lot of the beginning experience was learning to accept that, as my label announced, I was a chaplain.

To become a certified chaplain, four training units have to be taken. Twice a month, I signed in at five o'clock in the evening and was the chaplain on call until eight o'clock the next morning. I slept with my beeper and often did not tumble into bed until half past eleven at night. The Emergency Room became a favorite hangout.

I had many interesting experiences counseling people. I remember well visiting a young man who had lost his foot because of diabetes. I was very cavalier telling him that he was going to be fine. I was very new at this. Now, I would talk differently to him. I would probably listen more. People in hospitals are often scared and need to talk.

During my second unit, I was much more relaxed, not trying to pretend I was God and had all the answers. I loved much of it, feeling very useful.

I sat a lot with a dying woman whose two daughters would visit her almost every day. The patient was great. Once when I entered her room, a daughter said, "Mom, Arlene's here." I felt really good, special, like the woman liked me and was happy I was visiting her.

Once a woman strung out on drugs was very quiet, yet signaled that she wanted me to stay. I was silent and started singing to her. I sang some nursery rhymes and simple songs that came to me. She smiled once in a while. That too was good for me.

I stayed with some daughters when their mother's life support was being removed. The nurse's aide told me she was dead, but the daughters did not realize it and were not told, so it was very dramatic for them.

There is so much pain and sorrow in the world of hospitals. Of course people get better too, but my role was giving comfort. It was always sad for me when someone I was regularly visiting died.

When my husband became too ill for me to continue, I dropped out of school. I have forty-two credits towards sixty for a master's degree as a Pastoral Counselor. I often wonder if I will go back to complete my degree. We'll see.

A Courier

In 1991 I saw an ad in the local paper for a New York City courier. It was part-time work, and when I called the phone number, I learned the office was in the next town. I went for an interview and got the job carrying passports for a religious travel agency. I would be working mostly on the Upper East Side and sometimes lower Manhattan. The passports were for people traveling for their churches and, occasionally, for vacations. Some were missionaries; some were teachers. I went into the office to get my assignment for the day: both delivering passports and picking them up from foreign embassies.

A man trained me for three days. He showed me the subway system, taught me where the rest stops were, and otherwise introduced me to the job. I worked three days a week, catching the nine-thirty bus in front of the office and taking the two-thirty bus back home.

I loved the work very much. I walked throughout the city, carrying my lunch along with the passports. When I stopped to eat, I usually bought a coffee or, if it was really hot, a water. The hot days were the worst and I remember thinking on one of these days that I would not be able to make it back to the Port Authority. (I did make it, but walking on 42nd Street was hard!)

My husband knew the city since it is where he worked all his life. I learned about the city and the subway system and was very proud of myself. Once when my husband was having a business lunch with a good friend at a restaurant I passed, I stopped in before he arrived. I left an inscribed book I had bought from a street vendor for him and paid for two glasses of wine. He and his friend were delightfully surprised.

I often carried a notebook because I am a writer and if I had wait time, in the subway or especially at the French Embassy where there was usually a line, I would write impressions.

Here are a few of the poems I wrote.

Seventy-Fourth and Fifth Ave.

At 5th and 74th today a taxi backs out of the street
It can't get through
And an old couple, old, in the '80s
Both tall, white haired,
Get out and holding hands, holding hands, mind you
Begin to cross 5th on their way to 74th.

How far do they have to walk?
A lifetime?
A millennium?
A block?

I sit wishing I were them
Old. Finished. Getting home in the city
Making my way with someone old
Like me. Holding hands
Before I die.

What?

Oh! How he babbles
On and on he talks
So much to say
So much to be said
He sweeps the messes
left by others
And he talks and talks
If you listen
He talks.
I stop listening
I did not expect
Conversation, friendship, connection.
I just said hi.

On Seeing a Homeless Man Sleeping

What does it matter
Where he sleeps?

A subway station
Is just as fine a place
As any other
When one is sleeping.

Isn't it?
Aye, "there's the rub"
It is the waking
That matters
Not the sleeping.

And so on he sleeps, contented
Hard to look at with his
Open posture, spread-legged on his back
Like a dog.
Dirty sneakers, soiled pants
The emblem of how he lives
On the mean and dirty streets.

He takes three spaces
Where people could sit.
Yet he's allowed to spread himself
In sleep.
Isn't he?

We can stand
We have beds to sleep in, don't we?

After all what does it matter
Where one sleeps?

We may all be sleeping right now
With our eyes open.

Lots of Poems

Written while couriering
Written while waiting
Written all the time
Like music in my mind.
Songs without noise.

Port Authority

Sitting in an eatery
Bus waiting
Drinking coffee at an uncleared table.
The man outside the window
Watched the pizza slice
Uneaten, dead on its paper plate
Hungry
Unfocused
Drinking my coffee, I watch him
Watching the pizza
Our eyes did not meet.

Wanting to feed him
To feed all the hungried
He moved away.

Later, another man,
Black like the first
Boldly pointed toward the slice
Looking at me
Watching him.

The owner scowled, gesturing,
Begone, beggar!
Don't offend my customers.

Our eyes met
My soul cried

We both laughed
As I handed it to him
On the paper plate, besides.

Recent Years (2000 – 2010)

Aspects of Love

I wear my husband's sterling silver bracelet with his army ID number. On the back is engraved February 2, 1952.

Is it love that presses me to wear it now before he dies, before I find it in his effects and wear it with much sadness and grief? Instead, I wear it now with joy that he is still here.

A favorite aunt had it made for him when he was a sergeant during the Korean War. He was shipped to Washington to go overseas, but never did, serving his army time in the States.

We are together almost fifty years. Do I love him? Is it simply habit? When I cook his meals, buy his favorite foods, sleep with him, what does it mean?

Once when our son asked me, "What is love?" as he was rushing out of the house, I firmly answered, "Behavior." I like to think I believe it. I no longer like the emotional overtones we give the word LOVE.

"Love one another," it says on a Jewish synagogue in New York City on the Upper East Side.

"Love one another," Christ reportedly said.

A tough word to write about.

The Fall

In February of 2006, my husband fell in our house while I was in the bathroom. He weighed over four hundred pounds.

He called, “Arlene!”

I asked, “What?”

He answered, “I fell.”

I had heard the crash and thought maybe he leaned on the card table and it fell, but no, it was him, not the table.

This was the second fall in less than a year and I dialed 911. The firemen came and picked him up with lots of negotiations about how and what to do. I watched him laying face down with his massive hernia hanging on the floor. A doctor had said over ten years ago, “It’s not life threatening, so we’ll let it go.” The hernia was the size of a soccer ball and now that he had lost some weight, it looked even bigger.

When the firemen got him on his feet and sat him in a chair, they asked if he wanted to go to the hospital, and of course, he said no, a gigantic mistake. The terrible things that began to happen were because of this fall.

He began slowly to get sicker and sicker, and we finally knew that he had to go to the hospital, against his wishes—he so hated being there. A daughter slept over to help me get him out of the house. He did not leave his chair for two days. Again, a 911 call, a stretcher arrived, and they laboriously carried him from the house.

He was in the emergency room for a while. After an overnight, he was transferred to the ICU. They pumped a pint or two of blood out of his stomach!

He stayed in the hospital three full weeks, never being moved from the bed. He was transferred to a rehab for physical therapy so that he could learn to walk again.

In his first week there, they sat him in a wheelchair. I remember walking into his room and being pleasantly surprised. "Look at you sitting up!"

Once he was pinched into a mesh harness to be lifted and transported to the wheelchair, and as he was hanging there, they said the wheelchair was too small. Then they suddenly said that they had to order a new wheelchair because he was so big. He stayed in bed for weeks until the family finally called a meeting and said that we were transferring him. The rehab people started working with him immediately, slowly teaching him to walk again. The first time he walked thirty steps with a walker. (I was there!)

Twice he was transferred to the hospital because of urinary infections. That's what they said but I was always skeptical of their reasons. (They need their money too. Have him stay his full term with his Medicare coverage, and if he has a few trips to hospitals, well, that gives them more time to bill for services, right?)

It only delayed his recovery.

When the Medicare ran out, our children said that, if he was home for only three months, Medicare would kick back in and he could go into another rehab to relieve me.

He came home in August 2006, and I could not send him back to a rehab.

So, because Jim tripped and fell, he was a semi-invalid. And I was the one caring for him.

Clearing a Desk

I am clearing out Jim's desk. I have stacked papers dated from 2003 to 2005 in the burn-in-the-fireplace pile. I come across a small leather book marked Loch Ness. It hung on our bulletin board. I open it to see many small papers. As I am rummaging through them, I find money: a fifty-dollar bill and four twenty-dollar bills.

I am furious. We have already found lots of money that my husband stashed. I found money in some books. Our son found money in my husband's closet. I am talking about thousands of dollars.

What was he thinking? Did he want me to be happy with so much cash in the house after he was gone? Did he forget he put the money where he did? He was an idiot as far as I'm concerned.

My kids will say, "Oh, Mom, be gentle. He meant well!" No, I cannot be gentle when money seems to mean so much in this day and age. How can I be gentle when I think he did not consider me a true partner with him or I would have known about all the money he was hiding? What, was I going to spend it rashly? Would I not continue my frugal lifestyle? What, Jim, what? What was going through your mind as you hid this money? When did you begin hoarding money?

Have I thrown any away in all the books I discarded from your library? Have I thrown away hundreds of dollars because of your stupidity or forgetfulness?

I feel certain you forgot that there was money hidden in the house. I'm sure, after Wesley arrived, you were content being so well taken care of. You must have been happy when he showed you how he had cleaned all the cobblestones next to the house that you had laid so meticulously on your hands and knees. You must have been contented when he was rubbing your lower back for long periods of time.

So what was it, Jim? And I hope I do not stay angry at you for too long. I will put the one hundred and thirty dollars in my wallet and enjoy spending it. Thanks.

Anger at Jim

I found in Jim's desk an old cloth that was screwed tight with wires. I had to use pliers to open it. Someone said maybe it's money. I had many fantasies as I unraveled it that (1) it would explode in my face and blind me; or (2) that it would be a powder that would slowly turn into a liquid to dissolve my fingerprints; or (3) the cloth, as I dismantled it, would reveal something so horrible that Jim felt the need to hide it, wrap it, disguise it, store it away until the end of time, or until a fire broke out and destroyed it, rather than have me see it, handle it, be a part of it.

And it was money! It was lots of money, and I learned that the cloth was fireproof. Why did he not tell me about it? Did he want me to find it after he had died?

I do resent that I was always so frugal, that I often felt his gifts to me—my pinky diamond ring, my red convertible, my full length black mink coat—were all too little and too late.

Damn you, wasn't I your partner? Guess not to be trusted too much!

Imagine

My house will sometimes smell of my husband's legs. His nurse said some people don't mind the smell; others are put off by it.

I gag on the smell when the bandages have not been changed in two days. Now there are five of us: wife, three children, and occasional nurse changing the bandages in preparation for when Medicare coverage ceases, and we will be doing it all the time by ourselves.

My house smells of illness. Imagine that.

I still need to imagine good stuff happening, happy stuff, not morbid or scary, not towers being demolished.

I have been a health nut most of my life and raised my children on whole wheat bread, wheat germ, and yogurts. Once my oldest daughter said that some kid at lunch asked her why she always had brown bread. I don't remember what she told him or even if she asked me if she could have white bread once in a while like everyone else.

I am knitting and just finishing a lovely belt for my seventeen-year-old granddaughter. There is fringe hanging on either end, and I have been beading it. I have some wooden beads picked up from a great bead store on Bloomfield Avenue in Montclair and also tiny silver pieces that say IMAGINE. I stood for a long time looking at the small silver doodads—LIVE, LOVE, TRUST, HOPE—and chose IMAGINE because of the John Lennon song that kept floating in my mind as I looked at the display.

My youngest grandkids are a real delight when they visit or I babysit them. Knitting for my grandchildren is such a pleasure for me. A beautiful blanket made years ago covers a teenager's bed. Pictures of my grandchildren in knitted sweaters bring my heart much pleasure.

If I feel an occasional melancholy, I know it happens sometimes, and my job is to keep moving forward, keep on with my knitting or writing projects.

Someone said knitting is a symbol of nurture. I suppose it is. It also calms me and I do enjoy working with my hands, listening to the television and looking up to see an interesting scene. My imagination is still pretty good, and I like imagining how some sweater or other item will look.

I knitted a few spa cloths, made of cotton with a small intricate design. I gave them as gifts and I sit on one when I come out of my shower. A friend who said she would never sit on it asked me to turn it into a small clutch purse, which I was able to do. I wonder if she ever uses it.

March 2006

Jim is entertaining his four daughters and one daughter-in-law for St. Patrick's Day today. He will order from Foodies and two of the girls will go to pick up the food and bring it back here. I will be with my friend at a movie.

This tradition started when his daughters were in high school; I was never involved. It was okay with me.

One year for Columbus Day, being Italian, not Irish like Jim, I treated my son and sons-in-law to a Charlie Brown's lunch. They all showed but one and I enjoyed it very much. I don't know why I only did it once.

I unwrap Jim's legs and they bleed badly. Jimmy will be wrapping him, and I cannot stop thinking about the bleeding and the pain when I removed his wrap.

The nurse did not put Adaptic (an expensive non-adhering dressing that protects soft and weak skin and is easily removed) on the back of his leg, so when I began pulling the wrap off, some of his skin came off too. It is a horrible mess, blood on the toweling and floor. He should be in a hospital or a nursing home.

It is getting harder and harder to care for him. This morning he could not get out of his chair. I need for someone else to be taking care of him. I have just finished wiping him, lots of bowel movement. How does he clean himself? It seemed to be days' worth of stool. How can the sun shine so brightly when inside this house pieces of a man's excrement are falling on the floor and into a wet rag? There are two people suffering here, how can the sun be so bright?

I cannot cry yet. I want to release my sadness or shout at the gods, the gods that watch over our foibles and laugh. Somehow the idea that this is all illusion comforts me. I think Einstein or someone brilliant said this is all illusion. Why is it so painful?

He is not eating. Our daughter Alice slept over, and today we get him into the hospital.

Servanthood

There were two times, yesterday and early today, that I heard the word “servant.” One was when a friend at coffee said, “I don’t want to be a servant,” referring to the life she has with her husband. The other was when I was reading a woman’s critique at my Write Group meeting, and she said she was on her way to servanthood with her bishop and had to leave early.

I said loudly and angrily to Jim last night that I did not want to be a servant. Afterwards he had problems breathing while he watched television, and of course, I blamed myself that what I had said had triggered his breathing problems.

Yet, here is a grown woman friend who declares she will be a servant to her bishop. What? Why? Why would anyone choose servitude? Yet I know my friend is talking about serving God. She will be serving God by serving her bishop, right?

So whom do I serve? And why was I so angry telling Jim that I did not want to be a servant? Was I angry because I know I really am one, serving Jim? I remember Bob Dylan’s song in the ‘80s about having to serve someone or something.

I was a servant, cleaning Jim after a bowel movement, caring for him, handling this whole house and its myriad happenings.

Today I tell Marianna, the young woman caring for Jim, that her last day here is tomorrow. I hope the new sleep-in I hired works out.

Coffee vs. Tea

When I first met Jim, he drank tea; the strong Irishman that he was, he was not much of a coffee drinker. I love my early morning coffee, not the taste so much as the habit of it.

I would make Jim tea when we arrived at my house after a date. I suppose my mother bought the tea. She was a hearty woman and I am strong like her, but I feel myself melting away more and more caring for him and his illness. He's home now and in a hospital bed.

There is a man called Nelson who cares for Jim. He washes him, cleans his bowel movements, and takes good care of him. Nelson likes tea. He comes from Kenya and owns a tea plantation there, and he often makes himself a cup of tea.

I like the taste of tea every time I drink it and always wonder why I don't drink it more. Habits die hard and, sometimes, not at all. I seem to be getting over my wine habit, although my sugar needs are hard to diminish.

I only drink three or four cups of coffee a day and some of that amount has to do with if I eat out or not. I have a list of the ten best foods, and tea is on the list along with blueberries, apples, turkey. Coffee is not listed.

So as I age I will drink more tea, a cup a day maybe, and also keep my coffee habit. A friend I eat with every week, along with ten others, is the only tea drinker in the group of us coffee lovers and, yes, she is Irish.

Happy Days

I walk my dog and think of happier days. I remember when it was exciting to be going away—to the Catskills with the family, to our new lake house, and longer ago, to the shore for a month. I would pack a picnic lunch, and we would stop right before the parkway turn off and have sandwiches, drinks, chips, dessert. Those were all happy times.

A friend and I were recently saying that one never knows when a happy time will be the last one. When was the last time we went to our property in the mountains? When was the last time we were all together at the lake? When was the last time Jim walked?

I remember the day back in March when he was walking and taking care of his own toilet needs. I remember even now so many months later.

All the happy times and happy days that you don't know have finished. They are gone, maybe never to come back.

Are these my happy times now? Will I remember these times after Jim is gone? I watch a noontime television show with him and try to feel happy about it. I am happy with friends. I am happy with others, especially women.

What happy times are still coming, are still in my future? Will they be very different? Yes, probably, but happy is happy, right? I have to believe they will happen. I have to believe I will experience some sustained happiness again.

Ramblings

She was stunned that her life had turned out this way. There was such great promise as a young woman, such passion for life. Bearing much pain in childbirth, believing that pain could be given up to God, in Christ's name, and that all poor souls in the world would somehow be better, happier, healthier, holier.

Rather than curse the God that would allow such soul-killing, excruciating pain, she pleaded "Have mercy" and spoke to the inscrutable deity that ruled her life as a young woman. The communion wafer became a solace, friend, crutch, and comfort although it could not save her from the devastation her life would present.

There was so much joy in her mania that she credited God with being really good to her most of the time. The insulin in her early twenties, the screaming her brains out, almost naked, in front of her three grown children, and the terrible phobia of spiders she also accepted gracefully as gifts from God.

So nursing her injured and handicapped husband seemed part of the game she was programmed to play while alive; the game set in stone when she was born; the path she was meant to travel to achieve sainthood, which she wanted more than anything.

Does this path have a heart, a book once asked her, and she was able to say yes, yes, it does. It has a sentimental heart, an emotional heart, a resentful heart, a profound heart, a joyful heart, a grateful heart, a weary heart, but a heart, nonetheless, in a bright and seasoned brain, a questioning mind.

She had a brain and a heart that understood karma slightly, that understood the Christ who understood longing and hunger and passion and addiction. She was addicted to life, to food, to the living of it all—the good, the bad, the awful, the ecstatic.

She was nearing what felt like the end of her life, although she was only sixty-seven and her parents and grandparents had lived long lives. Now that she was ferrying her husband back and forth to doctors and to hospitals, she wondered when her great and happy life would begin again. She had known joy and happiness and so wanted to be rid of the chores and angers of her life today.

How could she do that? Would she do it? Would she turn her back and sing "So long, it's been good to know ya"?

No. No way would she gather the courage to walk away from her husband and her life right now.

She did believe that happiness would be hers again, just not right now.

Up All Night

My husband's whistle wakes me at two thirty in the morning. He needs something. I struggle from the bed and go to him. He lays on a hospital bed in our family room. Often the television is on as I attend to him, but tonight there is quiet and dark except for a small lamp in the adjoining room. He likes a light on at night now that he is approaching his death. He does not seem to know he's dying; only his doctor, the nurses and I know that the end is fairly near. He probably suspects but does not talk about it.

How soon I wonder, as he tells me he needs a bedpan. *O Lord, this means staying awake until I can clean him.* He sometimes sits on the pan for an hour.

When he was first home, he could not sit longer than ten minutes before it started pressing into his thin skin, hurting him. Now he's used to it, and so I turn the television on to amuse myself or to help me fall back to sleep until he calls me. The sofa is comfortable; there have been many nights when I have slept on it all night.

I do remember once saying to him that I could never respond to being whistled at, but then what else can I do? There are many nights that I sleep fitfully on the sofa to be close to him.

I was silent as I cleaned his bowel movement last night.

He didn't want dinner. Should that sentence go into his journal or mine? We are so linked for fifty years. Who knows? I threw away a friend's postcard from Florida, where she is golfing and swimming and having a good old time. I feel horrible towards her; she seems so insensitive to my plight.

Anna, who comes to give me a break now and then, came and slept here last night. Soon Jimmy's kids will be here, a good distraction for me. Anna never used the Hoyle lift so I will have to show her how to use it. I hope I remember.

I am depressed this morning. I was in the basement when I heard his whistle. He needed the bedpan. Then he asked for tea! I wonder about my commitment here. Is he not in a nursing home because my heart couldn't stand it or is it because it's too much money? Heart, I think.

Whatever it is, I am so weary of what has happened to us that I am slowly losing my mind. I am repeating myself the way Howard Hughes did in the *Aviator* movie. And what of the prayer I used to say, "Bless me into usefulness." Now what? Am I being useful to Jim? Is that the game here? My prayers are always answered?

I write here my rage and depression and anger and tiredness. But what will I be doing when he is dead? What will I be doing?

I cannot think about what my life will be without my duties. Do I define myself by my duties? Yes, to some extent.

Another awful thing—I forgot the very wet and smelly piss pads last night, and so this morning, I took a small bag to the street for garbage pickup (thank God I made it on time!) and then washed the two very wet towels. They had to be done, and I am disgusted with myself for having forgotten them last night when I took the garbage out at eleven o'clock.

So what the hell was that about yesterday, writing a suicide note? But I have nowhere to turn. Will the woman coming today to care for Jim speak English? Will she be able to move him, he's so big? What is going on here?

I am planning soon to sit in my garage with the two cars running. I think it will be painless. (What else do I think about it? I will fall asleep and not wake up. My spirit may wake in another dimension.)

I am worried, however, about the effects on the family. "My mother killed herself," the children will say. "My grandmother killed herself," some of the older grandchildren will tell their friends, maybe a teacher, a guidance counselor. "My friend committed suicide," friends will say, appearing shocked. "She was very depressed taking care of her ill husband."

None of them heard my cries of UNCLE. None of them had a solution for me.

God has been showing me how tough I really am, how really strong and disgustedly hard it is for me to say I have had enough. I cannot do this anymore, and the only way out I can see is killing myself.

I call Jimmy and he is coming over. Can I ask him to spend the night, change his father's diapers like he changes his son's?

Help, I say, help. I do not seem to have the ability to admit to my children that I have reached my end. How hard this is for me, how terribly hard.

The kids have volunteered to come here twice a month. Of course, my mentioning that I wrote a suicide note helped. (I did write one to have on hand in case I suddenly decided to end it for myself.)

Jim asked about getting out of bed this morning and I said no. He was furious at me. He sits now on a bedpan.

My daughter, Jeanne, is here with Nicole, her dog.

Ambrose from hospice came to talk about the "end stages of life." Jim was quiet. Ambrose mentioned that Jim complained that some of us do not seem to want him to get better. Was he referring to me? Please God take him gently. "Do not go gentle into that good night." Why not, I say. Why not?

Four of his five children came to celebrate his birthday. We had Hot Grill hotdogs all the way from the restaurant and I took some pictures of him becoming seventy-six.

Jim slipped out of bed yesterday when I was not here. He was lying on the floor with his head caught under the metal of the bed. I eased his head out and we rolled him over so that we could put the Hoyle lift under him in order to lift him back into bed.

Hard work, he is so heavy.

I wrote this while sitting in my car waiting for a train to pass:

After Jim is gone, I will:

1) buy a Mustang convertible

2) empty the house and sell it

3) spend lots of time at the lake

4) lose some weight and maintain one hundred fifty

5) swim three times a week and bike for exercise.

Jim and I had a big fight. He was hallucinating about a big chair from outside and wanted me to bring it into the house. He woke me twice just as I was falling asleep. He yelled that he wished I died and I yelled the same back to him. I was exhausted. I had interviewed Michael from New York for a sleepover position, but he did not want the job.

Jim is losing it more and more, last night asking that I remove his leg bandages. I cannot use the air conditioner in the bedroom because I might not hear his whistle, and so I sleep on the sofa all night.

I have read the hospice pamphlet the nurse gave me; it's excellent. I will make copies for the kids so they know what to expect.

When I dealt with my dad's illness, it was easier for me because he lived five minutes away and had a caretaker. I resented my brother because he lived in Ohio and did not help. I wanted it over for my dad—die already, die. His life was confined to his bed. How shocked I was when I pulled his sheets back and saw how emaciated he had become; he looked like a holocaust survivor. Compared to my dad, Jim is a big man, although his face is thin.

I have to call someone. Jimmy is in Long Island and Peg's at the lake; I feel lost and alone.

Jim could only walk to the bookcase yesterday. The social worker from hospice came late and Jim was sleeping. He left, said he'd come back, who knows when. He seems nice, but stupid.

I interviewed Wesley yesterday and asked him to start Sunday.

Wesley came last night about four o'clock and, so far, so good. Last night he swept the lower and upper deck. It is quiet now at 6:00 a.m. I woke at 4:30 a.m. and could not fall back to sleep. I meditated for a while, and it calmed me.

Jim is doing okay, but this is hard for me watching him die. I am always asking myself, "Is he dying?" Is there something we could be doing to keep him alive? Am I wishing him dead too soon? Then I will be free! My therapist, whom I started seeing when Jim got so bad, said write Jim a letter if I cannot talk to him about our life together, our more than fifty years.

Is it too soon for Wesley if I leave the house for a few hours? We'll see.

The children came Sunday for a meeting. I set a nice table, and Jimmy brought bagels. They inferred that I should be extremely nice to Wesley because it is somehow my fault that the other sleep-overs left.

A daughter said I am too sad and morbid and she does not like visiting here. I was hurt, but did not respond that my life has shrunken to a man in a bed. They want me to go on anti-anxiety pills, but I am refusing.

I spent an overnight with four others at a friend's house in the country. There was one bathroom in the seventeen-hundred-year-old house. We saw the Boston Pops, and I slept through the night until half past six. It was fun watching them put a lawn mower together.

Jim seems to have revived from his devastating sleeping/groggy/losing it experiences of last week. What is happening here?

I did not change him this morning even though I knew he had shit a little. He was okay until the hospice nurse came at eight o'clock. He almost fell when he was standing and slumped towards the sofa but I pushed him hard to get the wheelchair under his body, and Judy, the hospice nurse, Jeanne, and I pushed him into it. I knew we would never have been able to lift him from the sofa if he had landed there; I would have had to call the fire department (again).

Wesley spent the day with his wife and son. Jim seems to be getting weaker; it's hard for him to sit up in bed, but he walks to the table.

Jim sat in his wheelchair for almost seven hours, and Wesley and I said, "Never again," because Judy was not paying the attention she should have. Jim sleeps and she watches television. We had to help her get him back into bed when she was leaving at four thirty.

Jim's foot doctor panicked at the swelling of his legs and so I called the hospice and doctors. I talked with DeBell; it was his father who sewed a daughter's toe when she cut it mowing the lawn and saved her from walking with a limp. The hospice nurse said, "Mrs. McCarren stays so cool; how come she is panicking now?" and I laughed and said, "You're right. The stupid doctor, who sees him only every other month, panicked me." Then I told them thanks for calming me.

I need to talk to more people. I swam at Kathy's. I still would like Jim to die soon, gently in his sleep; please God. Help me to understand your ways even as I doubt you even exist.

Why do I have nothing to say to Jim?

How come we can't say that we are waiting for him to die to free us all from hurt and fear and anger and regret and pain? How come?

I am now sleeping on the sofa every night. He wants someone close. I will ask Wesley to sleep here a few nights a week.

I am weary of this life of mine. He has been home for over a year and I often debate whether I can put him in a nursing home so that I do not lose my sanity.

Jim came home from his rehab on August 12, 2006, and on August 11, 2007, I interviewed and hired Wesley for the job of live-in caregiver for Jim. Hospice service had started in July, and there was a nurse every day for four hours.

Wesley stayed until Jim died. I can still remember his

saying in October that Jim had only five-to-ten days because "His kidneys are shutting down; he's not putting out much urine." I was standing in the kitchen, and although I knew Jim was dying, I was stunned. Jim died a week later.

Day-By-Day

Friday, October 12, 2007

I had planned to go to the lake, but it was rainy so I went to an OA meeting in Passaic and got home about eleven o'clock. The plumber at the lake had called so I left at noon with Buck and arrived in Dingmans at half past one. He fixed what was wrong with the pump and left at four o'clock. I had planned to stay overnight (I don't like to make the trip in one day), but something was telling me to drive home. It was a nice drive, other than the heavy Route 80 going-home-from-work traffic backup. I arrived home at half past six and immediately went to Jim. Wesley was surprised because I had told him I would be staying overnight.

I sat on the bed near the window and told Jim that the plumber had fixed the pump and that I came home, instead of staying overnight, to be with him. Jim quietly responded and seemed happy.

Saturday, October 13, 2007

I went early in the morning to another OA meeting and told Wesley to tell Jim where I was. I bought bagels because Jimmy said they were coming over for the day; I also bought cappelletties and chicken broth.

I found the Notre Dame game on the television, and was

pleased to tell Jim (who in hindsight was out of it all day) when we put the game on at three o'clock. We all ate and never asked him if he wanted anything. He was sleeping so much.

Around six in the evening, I heard him throw up. It was dark fluid, black really. He was coughing up lots of phlegm and I got scared. *Please, God, don't let him die drowning.* I called Wesley, and he took off Jim's shirt and cleaned his mouth and chest. After Wesley removed his shirt, he got quiet and seemed to be sleeping. Jim stayed bare-chested all night.

That night, I was sitting on the sofa as Jim waved his left arm in a welcoming gesture. Over and over he slowly moved his arm towards himself. He seemed to be sleeping, maybe dreaming. I like to think that he was seeing his dead loved ones and inviting them to come to him.

Sunday, October 14, 2007

Sometime during the night as I slept on the sofa—he always wanted either Wesley or me sleeping near him—I heard him give a heavy sigh and cough almost as if he was disgusted with something. He did not call me and I did not hear him gagging or choking; I fell back to sleep.

I woke at 6:50 a.m., which is late for me to be sleeping. My first thought was that I was happy I had slept so late. I sat up and looked at Jim and knew he was gone. His mouth was open in that unique kind of stiff circle the lips make. My father had looked the same. I touched him, called his name, put my hand over his mouth, laid my head on his chest, and felt really strange. *Is this really happening, is he really dead?*

I went to the bathroom to pee. As I was coming back into the den, Wesley came towards me and said, "He's gone."

We looked at him and commented on how peaceful his

face looked. I called our son, only four miles away, and the rest of the children. They came quickly and stayed talking to him and ministering to him in their own styles. We talked about leaving him the way he was until Jeannie arrived from Rochester but decided that waiting for those few hours would be too stressful, so I called the hospice nurse, who came and pronounced him dead. She left papers for me for the funeral parlor, and I kept hesitating to call as we milled around, finally going outside—a nice, sunny day, warm, actually, for October.

Then it was time. I wanted his body with me for as long as possible. I knew the next time I saw him, he would be prettied up lying in his casket and I was not quick about wanting him to leave the house he loved so much. When I finally called, I told them he was a big man and they would need a few strong men to carry him. *A few good men.* It was a quiet time for us all.

The funeral people said it would be better to stay in another room while they removed him from the bed. I watched from the living room window as they walked him down the lawn. He was in a brown body bag being taken to the hearse. I thought *Look what a big man he was* without any shame or fear, but only with awe and gratitude. *Look what a big man I had the privilege to love and serve.*

Tuesday, October 16, 2007

It's early and we will be seeing him this evening for the first showing. I know your spirit is still here, Jim. I love and loved you.

Thursday, October 18, 2007

So here we are at the day. It's okay. *Please, God, make it okay.* I keep thinking of those last days. What did I do? What did we talk about? Did we talk together at all? On Saturday I ran out, visited with Jimmy and then Jimmy and his family came for soup. He seemed out of it. I don't want my memory to fade. CAN WE DO IT AGAIN? Can we? Can we prepare and do the funeral day again? Can I see him once more? Can I feel proud of my children and Jim's friends? Can I start at the first time I saw him on the beach in 1956? Can we do our lives over again one more time and make it more perfect than it was? Can I feel good being dressed in my navy blue outfit? Can I? Please? Whom do I ask? Tell me, whom can I ask to get permission?

And the response is, "Live in the moment. They go by in a flash."

Sunday, October 21, 7:15 a.m.

Yesterday, I made ravioli for Jimmy and his family. My friends, Paula and Chiz, came, then Alice and my granddaughter Melissa showed up after we had eaten. While we were eating, Peg called and I did not answer the phone. I felt sorry for her and then when I listened to the messages, heard Kathy had also called. I will call them both today.

Jimmy and the girls walked to Jim's grave with Paula and Chiz. It's eerie having the body so close, but nice. I am sure harder times are coming to me, but maybe not.

I hear Jeannie emptying the dishwasher. It is sweet of her. I want to offer Wesley less money, but I am nervous. I will sit with Jeanne outside, maybe; it's cold out.

Monday, October 22, 2007

So the funeral was great—sad, some weeping, but nice.

Jeff said at the graveside, "This is Shangri-la. Is that Grandpa's windmill?" He did not come to the repast.

It's over and I will not write anymore my impressions of Jim's decline and death, started so long ago in April of 2005.

As I say goodbye to Jim's journal, I know in my heart, I did well. He died as he wanted: in his beautiful home, visited by his children, and being served by Wesley and me at the end.

THANK YOU JIM FOR LOVING ME. GO IN PEACE. GO WITH GOD.

View from our back yard of the cemetery where Jim is buried

Remembrances

The first night after Jim was buried, Alice wanted the outside bunkhouse light on, and I groaned and fussed and told Wesley that, after the kids leave, we can turn it off. As Peg was leaving, she saw the light on and came back crying.

I fell asleep on the sofa and woke at 2:00 a.m. to go into my bed. When I got up, there, in all the darkness of the cemetery, was a light! I gasped in the loveliness of seeing that light. I cried. I like to think it is Jim's light, still shining. Thank you, Wesley. Thank you, Alice. Thank you, Jim, for putting the light on the bunkhouse so many years ago.

I walked Buck in the cemetery yesterday and he actually sniffed in the hole where you are. Oh my, am I going to start writing to you instead of about you? It seems surreal that you are gone.

Are you proud of how we have all handled ourselves so far? Are you proud of me? Thank you for loving me, Jim.

So now what? Maybe Jimmy and his family will come over today. Alice left last night. I took Nicole, Jeanne's dog, out on her leash, and she slipped out of her collar and ran into the cemetery. I panicked but she came back as I was going towards the house. It was still dark out at 5:45 a.m.

So much work to do around this house.

Journal Afterthoughts

Dogs

The dog does not worry if he leaves a toy lying in the middle of the floor. He does not worry about some clumsy adult tripping on his toy. He could care less if you are infirm, unsteady on your feet, using a walker or otherwise awkward. He drops his toy wherever he wants and whenever he wants. He goes happily about his business until next time, when he will pick up his toy to carry around for awhile.

What else can I say about this memory of my life lived with three dogs?

The first dog was my companion as a teen: a small puppy to sneak into the movie theater, to take on bike rides, to take swimming in a clean local river during the '50s. A puppy growing up until I was in college and no longer interested, then given to an uncle on his farm, hit and killed by a car on a highway that ran by the farm, but having a good and long life. The farm was in the very junction where Willowbrook Mall in Wayne, New Jersey, now stands.

The second dog was a magnificent German shepherd that was taken from its mother as a young pup. It sat on my lap in the back seat until it needed to get down and throw up. How smart, even then, the basic instinct to not mess oneself or environs.

Our oldest daughter had a good friend whose name was Toni Anne. All our daughters' middle names are Anne, after Jesus' grandma. So we decided, driving the dog to our home, to call her Toni Anne. She was a splendid dog, but sometimes, "Toni" sounded too male and not up to her standard of beauty and dignity.

After my mother died so suddenly, so completely, we were able to put Toni down fairly easily. She was beginning to mess in the house because she couldn't get out fast enough. Our vet said she had had so much dignity all her life that she needed to go out with her dignity intact. Thank you, Doctor. So we put her to sleep and she is buried in our backyard, a loyal and true companion for fourteen years.

Now this third dog of mine is a mixed breed, husky and shepherd, with one white eye and one brown. Rescued from a shelter at nine months, he is also a splendid dog, but he does drop stuff when he gets bored with it. And now that my husband is invalided, it can be dangerous. But then my husband's fall has already taken place. The fall has already done its damage. Who knew? Who knew what devastation that fall five months ago would have done? My husband, still not home, still in a rehab, still not able to walk with any strength yet.

Do I write also about my angers and resentments at his illnesses all these many years? The trips to hospitals, the wound care units, the doctor drives, the doing for him. I am only now beginning to realize what a caregiver I have been. I do not think of myself as a caregiver. A writer, a mother, a wife, a teacher, and now a grandmother nine times over. But a caretaker? No, not me. I have more important things to do than take care of a man.

I took care of five children, while he was out having some good times. Yes, he worked hard and earned our livelihood, but he also had some mighty fine times while I bathed and nursed HIS children to whole adulthood. I recall his three-month trip around the world, his going to Maine for the weekend with his bathing suit, the two times he was in Disney World, Florida, and I haven't even seen it once.

I can research my journals to find all the other good times he had without me while I tried to create my own good times without him. I did, too. I took journeys alone, looking in the dead of night for lake houses to be with friends. I went on a bike ride with others I did not know. Jim was not interested. (In fact as we got older, one of the awful things about our love was that he grew less interested in most things and not interested in what I liked.) I even bought a three-hundred-dollar bike that I have ridden just once.

I bought a moped once from a friend, and both my husband and son scared me into not using it. They were afraid for me, but why did I listen to them and not trust my own good instincts? I have always had healthy instincts.

Years later this same man asked to buy his moped back for his son to use. We said he kept his moped with me rent free!

So now my best companion outside of this house is my great dog, Buck. He and I walk in the park. I sit and watch him playing with other dogs in the doggy playground. I feed him and enjoy watching him romp with a daughter's female German shepherd. He has been the best, being gentle with a three-year-old granddaughter the very first day we brought him home from the pound when I didn't know him.

Aren't dogs the best?

The Buckster

He was such a magnificent dog that she often wondered how she could be so lucky. He came with papers written by his former owner praising his disposition and his loving nature.

But then maybe she was too old to appreciate him completely, for when he lifted his leg upon arriving in his new house for the first time, she was unsure whether she would want to keep him. She scolded and then gave him a hard biscuit to chew. When she went to take it away from him, he growled at her, sounding ferocious. She smacked him lightly on the nose saying, “No,” and pulled it away from him. That seemed to set the tone, and he was her loving dog and companion after that. He knew she was the pack leader.

He was half husky and half shepherd and had one white eye and one brown. When children would ask, she always said his mommy was a husky and his daddy was a German shepherd.

She and Jim decided to name him Buck, since it is the first word in *Call of the Wild* and was her husband’s favorite book. But she said if his formal name was Buckley, she would agree. It was hard for her to imagine yelling “BUCK! BUCK!” at the top of her voice when he got away from the house. But she learned to accept the name, and he was Buck until he died at her daughter’s house while she was in Florida.

Her grandkids petted him as he was dying, lying on his side, and talked and murmured to him. They put all their stuffed animals around his body when their parents were taking him to be cremated. It was a lovely image for her to see in her mind's eye.

He had a better death than if he were with me alone in this house.

Best friends always called him The Buckster.

To Our Dog, Toni Anne

I shall write before Toni dies. I love you Toni Anne. You have been a magnificent dog for fourteen years, a loyal and loved companion and friend. I am sorry that we have made the decision to put you down. Do not feel bad about your accident inside the house when you could not get outside fast enough.

Remember all our good times. You swam often in the ocean when we were vacationing there—always after 5 p.m. And remember the fun you had playing with Alice's dog, Woofer, when she visited.

I shall miss you always.

I sat in my chair in the den while she lay in her spot behind me, napping, always loving me, quiet, not knowing that these were her last hours. How could she know? She loved and trusted us.

I held her head murmuring love phrases to her as the doctor injected her. I felt her instantly gone. She was shaking; she was dead.

She is buried deep in our backyard in a special box made for her by friends, covered with a beach towel that she loved.

Go with God, dear friend.

Lake Living 2000

In 2000, I saw an ad for a lakefront house being built in Dingmans Ferry, Pennsylvania. The house had three bedrooms and two bathrooms.

The first thing I did was look at a map to see where Dingmans Ferry is; it is about three miles from the Delaware River. I asked a friend to go with me to see the house. She has a second home, and she loved this house. I brought my camera, and when I showed Jim the pictures, he was interested in seeing it.

Jim liked it a lot. He had grown up in a lake town in New Jersey and so knew the life. We contracted with the builder for extras, like a ramp for Jim since he had difficulty with stairs.

Jim often said that we should have done this ten years earlier. He loved working the small property and moving rocks to make a border along the properties.

We put all our children's names on the deed, so that when we both died, our children would not have to pay inheritance income taxes.

The first few years, we had great times there. I have many pictures of happy events: rowing our boat, burning logs in the gas fireplace,walking on the "water" in the winter, seeing Santa Claus on a December weekend.

As Jim grew weaker, it was hard for us to be there by ourselves. Sometimes he would not leave the house at all. I would order food and pick it up for us; we would sit on the deck hearing the silence, and we would enjoy it. It was always nice when a daughter or son was there because the grandkids loved it so.

The sandy swimming beach was three houses away, and we would walk to the beach to swim in the lake. We could swim off our deck also, but heavy sneakers were needed for the icky, oozy mud bottom. When you found a big rock, it was heaven to stand on.

Lake Experiences/Impressions

Friday, August 17, 2001

Just came out on the deck to wait for Jimmy and Joyce, my daughter-in-law. It is quiet here. The leaves rustle and the only other sound is a plane faraway and a dog barking faraway.

Saturday August 18, 2001

It is nine thirty-ish and we wait for my daughter, Kathy, and son-in-law, Bill. It is so incredibly quiet and lovely here. I am sitting at the deck table, writing. The ducks swimming by called a few times, maybe asking for bread. The interrupting sound of a large truck, maybe a bulldozer, across the lake is short; its motor slowly receding and quieting, probably stopped at its destination. It's the contrast that helps us to appreciate the quiet vs. the noise. Too much of one thing becomes boring, monotonous, trying, tiring, soul-killing.

Thank you, Creator, the Higher self within me and within Jim that said yes to this, that said okay, we'll take a chance, we'll do it.

A slowing down is what this allows, a stopping to listen, to enjoy, to let go of the sense of urgency that compels me when I am home: the urgency to accomplish (before death?), the urge to be published (before death), the urge to love life more deeply, be conscious for more minutes and seconds of the fleetingness of it all.

September 2002

A houseful yesterday. There were ten of us and Jack dropped off his sailboat. Jeanne's dog, Nicole, and our dog, Buck, romped and played—really best friends.

Walking Buck yesterday, a yellow cat started following us. I was nervous because Buck wasn't aware of the cat for a while, but when he turned, they sniffed at each other. Someone said the cat probably lived with dogs. It was nice.

Milford, a lovely tourist town, is eight miles away. We go for the restaurants and the large Grand Union.

December 2002

Three of us ladies are here with grandkids to see Santa. He arrives at the clubhouse and gives each of the kids a gift, while we all eat pancakes and bagels and drink coffee, lots of good, hot coffee. It is fun for us all.

At the Lake 2007

I open a small bottle of red wine and watch the storm start on the lake. We arrived here just as the rain started. There is light thunder in the distance and it's hard to know if it is coming this way or is moving away.

A huge and fat yellow-bellied spider made her web in the upper corner of the sliding door. I spotted her, feasting on a small insect caught in her large web, before I walked into her. I opened the door for Buck to go out and chose to stay in the house. I quickly got my trusty broom and pushed the spider away, out onto the deck.

The first job I always do when I arrive is to get the broom and sweep away all the country spider webs, and other debris that nestles under the outside eaves. I like the ceiling outside and the siding facing the lake to be clean of icky stuff. I am a city woman after all.

Once friends were frightened by a snake that had wound itself into a circle on the lawn near the lake. The man would not come off the deck, he was so frightened. The snake was molting, I'm sure and we got rid of it with our trusty broom. Someone who lives here year round said that it was a water snake and not harmful. Country living! My nemesis is spiders, not snakes!

The thunder is very distant now, storm moving away, just a trace of the sound, lovely.

Wesley called and is glad I am "doing things." The wine has mellowed me somewhat. It is quiet, quiet, thunder gone.

I am alone when Jim sleeps. Once I wrote a poem about Jim spending so much of his life sleeping. It is like he is dead, certainly to me, when he sleeps. It is like being dead, certainly to others, but not to the person sleeping. That person often will wake refreshed.

I nap for ten minutes and wake alert.

I miss being here with any of the kids or even friends. But it is lovely here—quiet, private, country living.

My Husband Sleeps

My husband sleeps
I want to shower
Yet not wake him.

My husband sleeps
Later than his usual
Waking time

My husband sleeps
I'll be leaving soon.

My husband sleeps
When I want him awake
For me.

My husband sleeps
I am confused.

My husband sleeps
I miss his wakefulness.

My husband sleeps
and I'm alone

My husband is not dead
Gone from me forever;
my husband is sleeping. June '97

Lake 2010

Now the house is not used as much as when it was new for us. Our children still enjoy it.

One daughter took her Girl Scout troop to the house for a weekend. The girls caught fish, rowed the boat, and had a marvelous time.

Best Friend

I have a friend of fifty years. I usually tell people she is the sister I never had.

We met in college, and the first time we met, she snubbed me, but she does not remember that. I understand now that she is not the snubbing kind.

We are not alike in many ways. I am a doer and like action. She is a romantic and likes fantasy. Although married, she and her husband never had children, while my husband and I had five.

She is timid, a small woman, yet she taught in an inner-city school all her working life. We think along similar lines about most things.

Now that we are both in our seventies, we joke about living together as widows. I usually say I could not handle her on a daily basis—always late and taking much too long to be ready to do anything.

My children wonder what we have in common. I tell them she is my best friend, that we tell each other everything, and that I find my heart in the heart of my friend.

My Eulogy at Jim's Memorial Service, October 2008

Dear Jim (Energy That Was),

Thank you so much for your hard and good work earning the money you did and leaving this planet and leaving me with so much money that I am occasionally careless.

Thank you, and help me manage my diabetes so that my eyes, kidneys, and feet are okay. I want to stay as healthy as I have been all my life into my eighties. I will have six to ten years. Not much time, but time enough to travel, enjoy the kids and grandkids, friends, maybe another man to love me.

I often wonder where you are, the time-old question of what happens after death.

I have learned recently about Energy. Some scientists said that they observed movement under the micro units. You showed me your calmness as you seemed to be welcoming dead loved ones, inviting them to come to you with your left arm moving in slow-motion—come to me, come here—over and over, gesturing slowly, over and over.

And then I heard your sigh, me asleep on the sofa near you. I listened to see if you might start choking, and no, it was a deep sigh, a strong exhalation of breath. I fell back to sleep, unusual for me. Was your spirit hovering over me, watching and guiding me back into slumber?

When I woke at 7:00 a.m., I saw that you were dead and that's when I realized what I had heard—your last breath.

Thank you, Jim, for loving me. Thank you, eternal Spirit, for giving me the great gift of Jim.

CPSIA information can be obtained at www.ICGtesting.com
Printed in the USA
BVOW011131071011

272761BV00007B/6/P

9 781935 751076